DECORATIVE Painting 1-2-3™

From Prep to Clean Up:

A Complete Guide

to

Interior Painting

Meredith.
BOOKS

TABLE OF CONTENTS

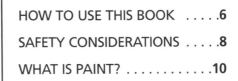

PLAN, PREPARE, PRIME, AND PAINT!

Most people who enjoy working around the house are willing, if not eager, to paint, and why not? The basics are easy to master. The materials are inexpensive in relation to other decorating projects and the results are evident in a matter of hours.

Painting is quick and easy decorating. Dollar for dollar, paint is the quickest, easiest, and most economical redecorating option. Changing the color scheme in a room will create an entirely different look and mood, help emphasize strong architectural points, and diminish those that are less attractive. Combining new colors and decorative techniques on the ceilings, walls, and trim will make your home come alive again.

So what's the catch? Nothing, really, just a little good advice. Success for any painting project results from careful planning, solid preparation and repair, priming and sealing before applying the final coat, and practicing unfamiliar techniques. In fact, 80 percent of the time spent on your project will be getting the surfaces ready for the final coats. The most expensive designer paint and the most striking decorative technique is wasted on walls that aren't properly cleaned and prepped. Preparation is so important to painting success that we've laid out the entire process from choosing color schemes, repairing and smoothing your walls, to applying the right primers and sealers in detailed step-by-step instructions.

OK, what about the fun part? We've got that too! Once the surfaces are ready we'll take you step-by-step through applying a simple coat of paint with brushes and rollers to more elaborate decorative painting techniques using special brushes, rollers, and plastic bags, newspapers, rags, and sponges to create beautiful and distinctive looks. Stippling, texture, ragging, faux leather, combing, color washing, and more are all inside.

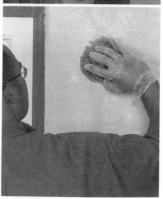

Painting is easy, fun, and satisfying. Let *Decorative Painting 1-2-3*™ help you get started.

DECORATIVE Painting 1-2-3™

Meredith Book Development Team
Project Editor: John P. Holms
Art Director: John Eric Seid
Writer: Charlie Wing
Contributing Writer: Sandra Neff
Illustrator: Jim Swanson
Designer: Theresa Cowan
Contributing Designer: Tim Abramowitz
Outline Development: Wade Scherrer
Copy Chief: Terri Fredrickson
Copy and Production Editor: Victoria Forlini
Editorial Operations Manager: Karen Schirm
Managers, Book Production: Pam Kvitne, Marjorie J. Schenkelberg
Contributing Copy Editor: Carol L. Boker
Contributing Proofreaders: Heidi Johnson, David Krause, Janet Anderson, Sue Fetters
Indexer: Donald Glassman
Electronic Production Coordinator: Paula Forest
Editorial and Art Assistant: Renee E. McAtee

Meredith® Books
Editor in Chief: James D. Blume
Design Director: Matt Strelecki
Managing Editor: Gregory H. Kayko
Executive Editor, Gardening and Home Improvement: Benjamin W. Allen

Director, Sales and Marketing, Home Depot: Robb Morris
Director, Sales, Special Markets: Rita McMullen
Director, Sales, Premiums: Michael A. Peterson
Director, Book Marketing: Brad Elmitt
Director, Operations: George A. Susral
Director, Production: Douglas M. Johnston

Vice President and General Manager: Douglas J. Guendel

Meredith Publishing Group
President, Publishing Group: Stephen M. Lacy
President-Publishing Director: Bob Mate

Meredith Corporation
Chairman and Chief Executive Officer: William T. Kerr

Chairman of the Executive Committee: E.T. Meredith III

The Home Depot®
Senior Vice President, Marketing and Communications: Dick Sullivan
Marketing Manager: Nathan Ehrlich

Image Studios/ Image I.T.
Account Executive: Lisa Egan
Set Building: Rick Nadke
Primary Photography: Bill Rein
Contributing Photography: Dave Wallace, John von Dorn
Assistants: Mike Steffen, Max Hermans
Stylists: Jill Wilmet, Mary Collette
Painting Consultant: Gregg Kranzusch
Production Manager: Jill Ellsworth
Account Rep: Cher King

Copyright © 2002 by Homer TLC, Inc. First Edition
All rights reserved. Printed in the United States of America.
Library of Congress Control Number:2001135118
ISBN: 0-696-21326-5
Distributed by Meredith Corporation

Note to the Reader: Due to differing conditions, tools, and individual skills, Meredith Corporation and The Home Depot assume no responsibility for any damages, injuries suffered, or losses incurred as a result of following the information published in this book. Before beginning any project, review the instructions carefully, and if any doubts or questions remain, consult local experts or authorities. Because codes and regulations vary greatly, you should always check with authorities to ensure that your project complies with all applicable local codes and regulations. Always read and observe all of the safety precautions provided by any tool or equipment manufacturer, and follow all accepted safety procedures.

Contact us by any of these methods:
1 Leave a voice message at **(800) 678-2093**
2 Write to **Meredith Books, Home Depot Books, 1716 Locust Street, Des Moines, IA 50309-3023**
3 Send e-mail to **hi123@mdp.com.** Visit The Home Depot website at **homedepot.com**

4 ROOM PAINTING BASICS   72–103

5 DECORATIVE PAINTING TECHNIQUES   104–175

6 CLEANING UP   176–185

INDEX AND RESOURCES   186–192

GETTING STARTED

IN THIS SECTION: what you should know

THIS BOOK IS FILLED WITH EVERYTHING you need to know for painting success! The tips and techniques will ensure beautiful painting results, whether you're an experienced or first-time painter. On the following pages you will learn how to use this book and discover some important information on painting safety.

LIGHT SOURCES AND HOW THEY PLAY OFF THE WALLS affect our perception of color in a room. The same color of paint will appear darker or lighter depending on the source and conditions.

HOW TO USE THIS BOOK

This guide to interior painting will get you started and help guarantee great results.

THE VOICE OF EXPERIENCE

WITH THIS GUIDE TO INTERIOR PAINTING, you can tap the expertise of Home Depot painting professionals from across the country. You'll find tips and techniques for everything from color selection to cleanup. How-to photos and step-by-step instructions will help you achieve spectacular results. Read the book from cover to cover, scan it for helpful hints, or zero in on specific details. You'll be entertained, educated, and most importantly, prepared to personalize your home with a fresh coat of paint.

Chapter 1: Choosing Colors defines primary colors, tints, and shades. It describes the effect of lighting on color, explores the effect of color on moods, and explains how to use paint chips in selecting color.

Chapter 2: Tools and Materials introduces supplies and equipment to help make your paint project as enjoyable as it is successful. It describes how and when to use brushes, rollers, and speciality paint applicators.

Chapter 3: Preparing to Paint explains how to plaster, clean, tape, and prime a room before applying finish paint.

Chapter 4: Room Painting Basics introduces techniques for painting walls, ceilings, doors, windows, and trim. A troubleshooting guide covers common interior paint challenges.

Chapter 5: Decorative Painting Techniques begins with recipes for latex glazes, the finish materials used in creating special effects. It demonstrates 20 popular techniques for glazing your walls to achieve a decor with artistic flair.

Chapter 6: Cleaning Up deals with drips, spatters, and residuals of a paint project. Read how to care for brushes and rollers, and seal leftover paint, as well as dispose of empty paint cans, contaminated solvents, and dirty rags in an environmentally safe manner.

The painting professionals at The Home Depot and experts at home centers and hardware stores are great resources for advice on projects and problems. Take advantage of their voices of experience!

TRICKS OF THE TRADE

TIPS FROM THE PROS at The Home Depot®: Their years of experience will translate into instant expertise for you. Look for these special icons, which signal detailed information on a specific topic.

TIME SAVER
Learn shortcuts that work.

TRIP SAVER
Save time and gas mileage.

CLOSE LOOK
Understand all the details.

TOOL TIP
Use specialty tools to their best advantage.

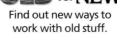 **OLD vs. NEW**
Find out new ways to work with old stuff.

 **WORK SMARTER**
Make smart work choices.

 GOOD IDEA
Learn what you need to know before you begin.

 **HOMER'S HINDSIGHT**
Avoid common mistakes.

 BUYER'S GUIDE
Select the best materials.

 **UP TO CODE**
Find guides for safer work and cleanup.

 SAFETY ALERT!
Prevent unsafe situations.

QUALIFYING YOURSELF

PAINTING A ROOM is an enjoyable, rewarding experience—indeed, it should be fun! And when you assess your skills accurately and honestly, it is. The key is to select projects that you can approach with confidence and complete successfully. Assessing your painting skills and interests before you begin is essential. Start by answering some questions:

■ **Do you enjoy painting and decorating your home?** Enjoyment gives you a rare edge over experience, particularly when you consult with the painting pros

at The Home Depot. Your desire, combined with their knowledge, is key to a successful paint project!

■ **Are you ready for some physical labor?** Washing walls, plastering and sanding them, and brushing and rolling on paint are repetitive motions requiring a

APPLYING A FRESH COAT OF PAINT is an enjoyable and rewarding project.

variety of forces. Your hands, wrists, arms, and shoulders may ache a little in the beginning, but just look at your project as the opportunity for a little physical exercise.

■ **Can you endure paint spatters?** Some painting projects, such as ceilings, are messy. Others inspire chaos. Most take longer than anticipated. Plan from the start to enjoy the chosen project one phase at a time. Then celebrate each completed stage.

■ **Will you practice new painting techniques?** Learn new painting and special-effect techniques in a closet or laundry room. When you're happy with your efforts, move on to more visible living and dining areas. This is a good way to avoid errors and dress up private spaces at the same time.

When you are comfortable with your answers to these questions, you're ready to paint! Consider starting with a simple project and grow into special effects, such as glazing, as your technique improves.

Rely on the painting pros at The Home Depot. They will help you select the best paint and tools for the project at hand. They will also give you solid advice on how you can achieve the best results.

FIVE STEPS TO SUCCESS IN PAINTING

THERE ARE FIVE KEY ELEMENTS to any successful painting project, whether it is the simple painting of a ceiling or following several steps to create a special effect.

1. INVEST IN QUALITY PAINT. It is easier to work with, covers better, and lasts longer. Important characteristics include adhesion, flow and leveling, ease of stain removal, scrub resistance, burnish resistance, lack of spattering, and resistance to sticking or blocking. Associates at your local home center will help you determine which paint is best for you.

2. INVEST IN THE BEST TOOLS. They make surface preparation and finish application easier and safer. Quality brushes and rollers hold more paint, produce a more even application, and don't leave bristles or lint that you'll have to fish out of drying paint. A good stepladder provides

a firm platform when a steady hand is needed. Painter's tape is easy to apply, and may be left in place for as long as one week prior to painting without tearing or lifting the underlying surface. Be sure to remove it right after painting.

3. PREPARE THE SURFACE CAREFULLY. Paint is an extremely thin coating; cracks, dents, and holes will show through unless you fix them before you paint. If the wall is moist, sooty, or greasy, the paint may eventually blister, peel, or stain. Not even the best paint can conceal a poorly prepared surface.

4. TAPE OFF THE ROOM AND COVER SURFACES THAT WON'T BE PAINTED. It will save you time in the long run—and give you better results. Edging will have a more professional look. You will be able to paint at full speed, with less concern for spatters. And cleanup will be faster: You won't have to scrape paint speckles, splotches, and drips from surfaces you didn't intend to paint.

5. PAINT UNDER THE PROPER CONDITIONS. To get the best results, follow the manufacturer's recommendations for maximum and minimum ranges of temperature and humidity.

SAFETY CONSIDERATIONS

Think safety when you paint, and protect yourself as carefully as you do your possessions.

POINTS OF PROTECTION

PAINTING SAFETY STARTS by taking care of yourself. When you're painting inside, keep these critical points of protection in mind:

■ **Eyes.** When you are scraping, power sanding, painting overhead, or spray-painting, wear plastic safety glasses or goggles to protect your eyes from flying paint droplets and particles. If you get something in an eye, rinse it out immediately with fresh water.

■ **Hands.** Many liquids associated with painting (thinners, removers, cleaning solvents, and bleach) are toxic or harmful to your skin. When handling these liquids, wear appropriate gloves: latex for latex paints and stains; neoprene for most solvents. Wear cloth work gloves when sanding, scraping, or using cleaning pads, such as steel wool.

■ **Feet.** Paints are slippery liquids. Wear shoes with slip-resistant soles.

■ **Lungs.** Two things to keep out of your lungs are solids and solvents. Paint projects generate both.

Sanding produces a fine powder, which is difficult to avoid breathing. The most dangerous dust is that from lead-based paint or from asbestos in older ceiling tiles that were installed before 1978. If you suspect lead (any paint purchased or applied before 1978), test it (see "Safety Alert", next page); if it is lead-based paint, do not sand it. When sanding paint that is not lead based, wear a tight-fitting, dust-resistant mask.

When you smell a solvent or paint, you are breathing it. Wear a respirator recommended for the solvent and be sure the space is adequately ventilated whenever you are working indoors.

■ **Clothing.** Wear old, loose-fitting shirts and pants. Put on an inexpensive, lightweight painter's cap to keep paint spatter out of your hair.

SAFETY PRECAUTIONS

THERE ARE SEVERAL PHASES of any painting project that require safety precautions and the right equipment for the job:

■ **Scraping, sanding, and wire brushing.** Protect your eyes from flying particles by wearing plastic goggles. Wear gloves to protect your hands from sharp scrapers and wire brushes. Protect your lungs from sanding dust by wearing a tight-fitting, dust-resistant mask.

■ **Removing paint with chemical strippers or a heat gun.** Work outdoors whenever possible. Otherwise, provide plenty of ventilation by opening windows on at least two walls and using a fan. Always wear a chemical fumes respirator. Protect your hands with

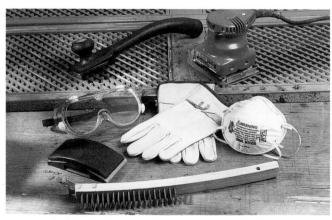

TOOLS FOR SCRAPING, SANDING, AND WIRE BRUSHING

TOOLS FOR REMOVING PAINT WITH CHEMICAL STRIPPERS OR A HEAT GUN

USING STEPLADDERS

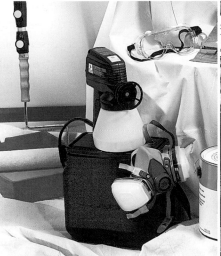

APPLYING PAINT

STORING AND DISPOSING OF PAINTS AND SOLVENTS

neoprene gloves. Keep children and pets out of range of the dangerous solvents and fumes.

■ **Using stepladders.** Make sure the stepladder is contacting the floor solidly on all four feet, or it may move unexpectedly. Before you stand on it, lock the ladder in the open position by pushing down on the braces until they catch. Never try to shift a stepladder while standing on it. Don't ever stand on the top two steps; if you can't reach what you're trying to paint easily you need a taller ladder.

■ **Applying paint.** Protect your eyes with goggles when you're painting overhead or using a paint sprayer. When you use a sprayer, double-check hoses and fittings, and check the spray in a safe direction. Wear a respirator when you use solvent-based paint, and turn off all pilot lights and other spark sources. To avoid spills, place open paint containers where you won't trip over them; keep children and pets away from the area. Wear shoes with slip-resistant soles.

■ **Storing paints and solvents.** Make sure paint containers are unbreakable and securely sealed with childproof lids. To reduce paint skinning to an absolute minimum, store the can upside down.

■ **Disposing of paints and stains.** Never dispose of liquid paint or stain with ordinary household trash.

SAFETY ALERT!

lead paint alert

IF YOU ARE SANDING or removing paint, especially if it is light-colored and applied before 1978 (it may be hidden beneath one or more top coats), test it for lead. Paint stores sell test kits that will reveal the presence of lead. Do not attempt to remove lead-based paint either by sanding or with a heat gun. Contact the Environmental Protection Agency (EPA) at 1-800-424-LEAD or www.epa.gov for guidance.

Instead, try to use leftover material by applying another coat. In some locations it is permissible to place empty or thoroughly solidified cans in the trash. Check with your local trash department before doing so, however. If permissible, paint can be dried by pouring vermiculite or cat litter into the can and leaving the lid off until the mass solidifies. Place the can in a secure location while it dries out.

■ **Always use adequate ventilation.** When you're working with solvents, thinners, paint particles, or dust from sanding and finishing, wear the correct respirator or mask for the project. Open windows and doors to provide adequate ventilation and to remove toxic vapors and particles from the work area.

WHAT IS PAINT?

Choosing paint involves more than picking a color. Understand the basics to make the best selection.

COMPONENTS

PAINT IS A THIN COATING designed to mask and protect the surface beneath. It usually consists of four components:

■ Liquid (water or mineral spirits), which allows the paint to be applied, then evaporates.

■ Pigments to give the paint color and hiding power.

■ Additives to modify the paint's characteristics.

■ Binder, the plasticlike material that binds the pigment and additives to the surface.

Liquid. The liquid for latex paint is ordinary water. In oil-based paints, it is mineral spirits (paint thinner).

Pigments for oil and latex. Pigments are finely ground, naturally colored solids that, when mixed, produce the desired paint color.

Prime pigments provide most of the color and give paint the ability to hide a color underneath. These include:

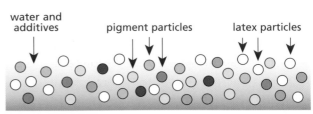

WET LATEX PAINT: particles dispersed in water

DRYING LATEX PAINT: water evaporating

DRY LATEX PAINT: latex particles fuse, entrapping pigment

AS IT DRIES, the water in latex paint evaporates, leaving a coat of protective latex and color pigments.

■ TiO_2 (Titanium Dioxide)—white.

■ Organic pigments—the brighter colors, such as phthalo blue and Hansa yellow.

■ Inorganic pigments—nonfading pigments, such as red iron oxide and brown oxide, ochres, and umbers.

Extender pigments are low-cost materials, such as clay, calcium carbonate, talc, silicas, and silicates.

Additives. These are chemicals added to the paint to enhance its mildew resistance, ability to stick to the surface, and to make it flow more effectively.

Binders. Most latex (water-based) binders are 100 percent acrylic or vinyl acrylic. Acrylic binders are used

PAINT SHEEN

SHEEN	BEST FOR	BENEFITS
FLAT	■ walls and ceilings (except kitchen/bath)	■ muted appearance ■ hides imperfections ■ best touch-up characteristics ■ better dirt resistance (eggshell)
EGGSHELL	■ walls and ceilings (can be used in kitchen/bath)	
SATIN	■ walls in any room ■ kitchen and bath ceilings	■ resists dirt better than flat ■ richer in appearance than flat
SEMIGLOSS	■ high-traffic area walls (kitchens, baths, etc.) ■ doors, trim, shelving	■ resists dirt and easily cleaned ■ not as shiny as gloss
GLOSS	■ doors, trim, shelving, kitchen cabinets, bathrooms, and wet rooms	■ resists dirt and mildew ■ easily cleaned ■ best water resistance ■ reflective—bright appearance

CLOSER LOOK

sheen and finish

SHEEN AND FINISH BOTH REFER to the reflective characteristics of the paint after it has dried (flat, satin). Painters use the terms interchangeably.

in exterior paints and primers and some premium interior paints because of their high adhesion (blister and crack resistance), water resistance (dirt and mildew resistance), and alkali resistance (fresh masonry). Vinyl acrylic binders are used in interior flat, satin, and semigloss paints, and in wall primers.

Oil-based (solvent-based) binders include linseed oil, tung oil, and alkyd. The first two are natural vegetable oils, while alkyds are oils that have been modified to dry faster and harder than regular oils. A negative of alkyds is that they harden with age and become prone to chipping. They are also being phased out because of their high volatile organic compound (VOC) content.

LATEX OR OIL PAINT?

LATEX PAINTS HAVE SEVERAL ADVANTAGES over alkyds (oils). Latex is flexible, thins and cleans up with water, dries quickly, and has nontoxic fumes. In exterior applications its ability to breathe water vapor reduces peeling and blistering.

Alkyds, however, have greater adhesion over smooth, nonabsorbent surfaces, such as plastics and metals. And they can hold a greater percentage of solids, often allowing single-coat coverage.

Sometimes the best solution is both: an alkyd primer for adhesion and hiding, a latex top coat. The question of which to choose may soon be academic, as the Environmental Protection Agency (EPA) and state authorities are increasingly limiting the use of alkyd (solvent-based) paints.

WHAT IS QUALITY PAINT?

THERE ARE REALLY TWO WAYS TO DEFINE QUALITY WHEN IT COMES TO PAINT. Every painting expert will tell you to buy quality (meaning good) paint. Quality paint provides better coverage, truer color, and requires less work to apply. But the word quality appears on almost every can of paint in the store, and labels don't really help define what makes a good paint. So how do you know you are getting a good product? The simple answer is price. Generally the more you pay, the better-quality paint you get. But there's another quality consideration as well. What do you need to do the job? People paint for different reasons. A family with kids who like to draw on the wall needs a paint that is durable and washable. A short-term renter is looking for low cost. A contractor wants a paint that is inexpensive and hides well. A decorator is looking for intensity and range of color. Let the people at your paint center help you decide what level of quality is right for you.

LATEX AND OIL (ALKYD) PAINTS COMPARED

PAINT TYPE	GENERAL ADVANTAGES	GENERAL LIMITATIONS
LATEX	■ cleans up with water ■ excellent color and gloss retention ■ good adhesion to many surfaces ■ breathes (allows moisture vapor to pass)	■ most are not applicable below 50°F ■ liquid paint may be ruined by freezing
ALKYD	■ good hiding ability ■ high adhesion ■ allows longer time to brush ■ good flow-out of brush marks ■ resistance to sticking (blocking)	■ flammability ■ yellows, embrittles, cracks with age ■ not for use on galvanized metal or fresh masonry ■ high volatile organic compound (VOC) content and resulting odor

fully cured or just dry?

THERE'S A BIG DIFFERENCE BETWEEN a paint that is dry to the touch and one that is fully cured, meaning that all liquid has evaporated and the color has reached maturity. A paint can be dry to the touch in several hours, but it can take as long as 30 days to fully mature and cure.

1 CHOOSING COLORS

IN THIS SECTION: understanding color

UNDERSTANDING primary colors, tints, shades, and tones helps you choose colors. This chapter describes color relationships and explains how to design eye-pleasing color palettes. Photographs and illustrations demonstrate the effects of light on color and color on mood. Details include how to use paint chips to select color.

COLORS ON THE WALLS AND TRIM WORK TOGETHER with light sources and accessories to create the mood and feeling of a room.

KEY QUESTIONS

You'll select color with more confidence when you answer some basic color and design questions.

BEFORE CHOOSING THE COLORS YOU'LL USE IN A ROOM you'll need to answer the same questions an interior decorator would ask:

■ **How permanent will this color be?** Use a bold palette if you plan to repaint in a few years; be more conservative when you are planning to sell the house.

■ **What is your decorating style:** country, Early American, Victorian, or contemporary? The colors and color combinations associated with decorating styles can serve as starting points for your color scheme.

■ **Which of the existing colors in the room will remain the same; which will change?** Is the carpet staying or will you change it as part of your new color scheme?

■ **Which furnishings and window coverings will stay?** Keep in mind when redecorating that it is far less expensive to change the color of a wall than to replace furnishings. Paint is your best decorating deal.

■ **How much natural light enters the room during the day?** Sunshine enters south windows much of the day. East or west windows receive direct sun only in morning or afternoon. North windows receive indirect sunlight. The type of light affects our perception of color (see page 22).

■ **What is the main source of light at night:** fluorescent or incandescent? Like daylight, the type of artificial light affects how we see color (see page 22).

■ **At what times of day will the room be used most?** Think about the lighting in a room when you'll be using it most, and select your colors accordingly.

■ **What are the dominant colors in adjacent rooms?** If another room is seen through a doorway, consider its color a part of the overall color scheme.

■ **Would you like to make the room appear larger or smaller?** Color can make a low ceiling appear higher or a high ceiling appear lower (see page 26).

■ **What mood are you trying to create?** Is this a space for quiet reflection and reading, a spot/space for unwinding after a hard day at the office, a room where you pamper yourself and prepare to face the world, or a workshop where you assemble intricate ship models?

The time and thought invested in answering these questions will be repaid many times in a home that reflects your personality and suits your needs.

DESIGN TIP

find a starting point

WHEN CHOOSING A COLOR SCHEME try to find a starting point to make the job easier. It can be your walls, floors, a favorite object or painting, or furniture that will be part of the finished room.

COLOR HAS POWERFUL EFFECTS on spaces and the people who live in them. That's why it is important that everyone who shares a space helps select its colors. Start by looking together at interior design books and magazines. Take note of pleasing colors and schemes. When you agree on a color scheme, match paint chips to the colors you like.

WHAT IS COLOR?

Color is the visual information by which people perceive their surroundings.

COLOR IS WHAT WE SEE when an object reflects electromagnetic radiation. The complete spectrum of electromagnetic radiation includes everything from long radio waves to short gamma rays. In the narrow range detected by the human eye (the visible spectrum), each wavelength corresponds to a pure color.

White reflects. White is not a single color; it's the reaction of the eye to the entire range of visible wavelengths. A white object is simply one that reflects all colors equally.

Black absorbs. Black is the complete absence of light. A black object absorbs all visible wavelengths. It reflects no color for the eye to detect.

The photographs below illustrate the impact of light on the perceived color of an object. The same green vase and white table are used in all three photos. Since a white object reflects all colors, the table always appears to be the color of the light source. Because a green object reflects only green light, the vase appears to be green when illuminated either by pure green or white light. When illuminated by red light, however, the green vase reflects no light and thus appears to be black.

This is why it is so important to judge colors under all lighting conditions in a room.

COLOR SPECTRUM

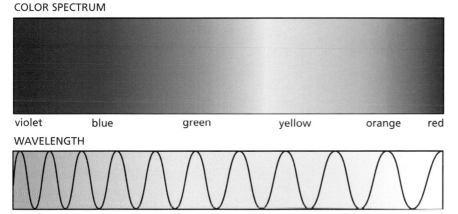

violet   blue   green   yellow   orange   red

WAVELENGTH

COLOR BLINDNESS

A NORMAL EYE responds to and can distinguish all of the colors in the visible spectrum.

Some people have eyes that lack receptors for certain wavelengths—red and green in particular. People who cannot distinguish between the colors are termed color-blind.

About 25 percent of males suffer some degree of color blindness. The percentage is lower for females.

A GREEN VASE and white table illuminated by green light.

THE SAME GREEN VASE and white table illuminated by white light.

THE SAME GREEN VASE and white table illuminated by red light.

THE COLOR WHEEL

When you understand the relationship between colors, you'll be more confident combining them.

THE COLOR WHEEL

A COLOR WHEEL ORGANIZES the visible spectrum of colors and shows the relationships between them. There are 12 pure colors on the most commonly used color wheel:

Three primary colors, red, yellow, and blue, are equally spaced around the color wheel. They are called primary because they cannot be derived by mixing other colors.

Three secondary colors, orange, green, and violet, are derived by mixing equal parts of the primary colors:

    red + yellow = orange
    yellow + blue = green
    blue + red = violet

Six tertiary colors result from mixing equal parts of primary colors with their adjacent secondary colors:

    red + orange = red-orange
    red + violet = red-violet
    yellow + orange = yellow-orange
    yellow + green = yellow-green
    blue + green = blue-green
    blue + violet = blue-violet

THE COLOR WHEEL defines the relationship between colors. Pure colors, those which have not been mixed with white or black, are on the third ring from the outside of the color wheel.

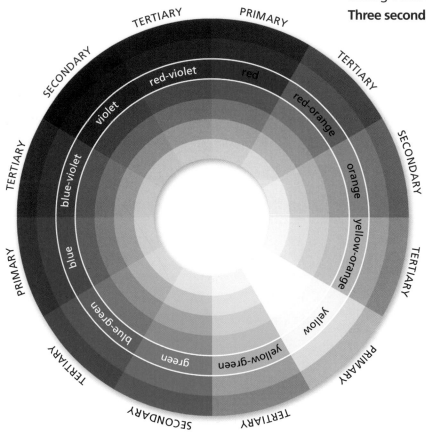

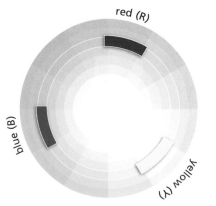

3 PRIMARY pure colors

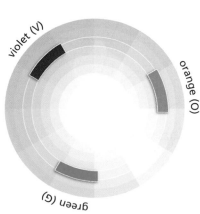

3 SECONDARY pure colors

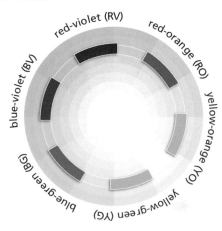

6 TERTIARY pure colors

BLACK AND WHITE
COLORS OUTSIDE AND INSIDE the ring of pure colors on the color wheel result from adding black or white.

Black is the absence of all light. Black paint absorbs all wavelengths of light, reflecting no light of any color. That is why the inside of a closet (no light) and a black object (no reflected light) are both perceived as black.

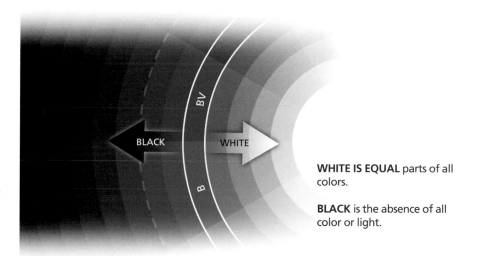

WHITE IS EQUAL parts of all colors.

BLACK is the absence of all color or light.

White is the presence of all colors. It is what the eye sees when struck by all colors of the spectrum, with natural sunlight serving as the standard source. White paint is white simply because it reflects all wavelengths of light equally.

Grays are mixtures of black and white. They are commonly specified as percentages of black.

DILUTING COLORS WITH BLACK AND WHITE:
TINTS, SHADES, AND TONES
PURE COLORS, which appear on the third ring of the color wheel, have not been mixed with black or white. They are almost never used in interior decorating except for emphasis. They are simply too strong. Instead, pure colors are mixed with either black or white.

Mixing with white. Mixing a pure color with white produces **tints** of that color—lighter versions of the same color, which appear inside the third ring of the color wheel. The more white is used, the lighter the tint, as shown by the increasingly lighter tints toward the wheel's center.

Mixing with black. Mixing a pure color with black produces **shades**—darker, richer versions of the color, which appear outside the third ring of the color wheel. The farther from the center and the higher the percentage of black, the darker the shade.

Mixing with black and white. Mixing black and white produces gray. The result of adding gray to a color is called a **tone**. The color appears toned down as if you were viewing it through smoke or fog.

USING THE COLOR WHEEL
With the color wheel, you can choose basic color schemes by :

■ Predicting the results of mixing equal parts of any two colors, as well as black and white.

　　■ Applying simple geometric rules to select pleasing combinations.

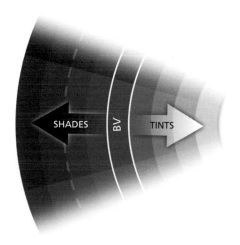

SHADES are mixtures of pure color with black. They seem darker than the pure color.

TINTS are mixtures of pure color with white. They seem lighter than the pure color.

BASIC COLOR SCHEMES

With the color wheel, you can design color palettes that are exciting or tranquil, bright or subdued.

A COLOR SCHEME need not be difficult to devise. You can use the relationship between colors on the color wheel to guide your selection. A factor to consider when choosing color is that lower grades of paint use black to help hide imperfections, which diminishes the intensity of the pure color. To get pure colors you'll have to use more expensive paint.

MONOCHROMATIC COLORS

THE TINTS AND SHADES of a single color are monochromatic. (For example, color cards usually show paint chips in a range of tints and shades for one color.) A color scheme using tints and shades of a single color is called monochromatic.

Use a monochromatic color scheme to create an aura of serenity, elegance, and unity. Monochromatic colors do not compete; they cooperate. The infinite number of tints and shades can provide emphasis and variety or can be used to focus attention on a particular object or area of a room.

Monochromatic color schemes are perhaps the easiest to implement. Select one color for a room. Next, determine which surfaces should be darker and which should be lighter. Remember that the farther apart colors are on their slice of the color wheel, the more contrast there is between them.

Start with white and add color. Monochromatic color schemes often work best starting from white. For example, begin with a white ceiling. Paint the walls in a slightly red tint (light pink). Paint the window and door casings and the baseboards a

THIS SLICE OF THE COLOR WHEEL shows all tints and shades of blue, creating a monochromatic color scheme.

BATHROOM BLUES. Note the interesting variety of tints and shades—all variations of a single color. A white ceiling would reflect the blue of the walls and furnishings, evoking a sense of airiness.

stronger tint of that same red. Create a tonal contrast for the doors and window sashes by adding gray to the color you used for the door and window casings.

TRIADIC COLORS

THREE COLORS THAT ARE EQUIDISTANT from each other around the color wheel are triadic colors. As you can see in the photo (right), a triadic color scheme of the primary colors can stimulate visual excitement. Triads of nonprimary colors are nearly as strong. They can create interest because they are unusual.

Use tints and shades. To moderate the visual excitement of a triadic color scheme, use tints or shades instead of pure colors. Select colors from the same ring of the color wheel either inside or outside the third ring.

The closer a color is to the center of the color wheel, the more restful it is on the eye. If a color combination is too dark, select lighter tints. If it is too light, substitute darker shades.

ANALOGOUS COLORS

COLORS THAT ARE SIDE BY SIDE on the color wheel are analogous, or adjacent.

The contrast between analogous colors evokes a feeling of greater depth than monochromatic color schemes. To add more depth, use a variety of tints and shades.

Stimulate serenity. Use an analogous color scheme when you want to create a softer, less intense atmosphere while maintaining visual activity. Use pure colors as accents, to emphasize a major design element, and to create visual movement.

Texture, pattern, and surrounding colors all work together to create the sense of harmony in an analogous color scheme.

THIS BRILLIANT COLOR SCHEME is based on a triad of pure primary colors. For less visual excitement, use tints or shades instead of pure colors.

THE COLOR WHEEL shows all tints and shades of red, yellow, and blue, creating a triadic color scheme.

BASED ON BLUE AND BLUE-GREEN, this color scheme (above) uses texture as well as tints and shades to create a color palette with depth and contrast.

THE COLOR WHEEL shows all tints and shades of blue and blue-violet, creating an analogous color scheme.

BASIC COLOR SCHEMES (continued)

COMPLEMENTARY COLORS

TWO COLORS POSITIONED exactly opposite each other on the color wheel are said to be complementary. Color schemes that use tints and shades of colors opposite each other are complementary color schemes.

You might expect that pairing colors spaced the maximum distance apart on the color wheel would produce discordance. On the contrary, complementary schemes are commonly found in nature, such as the red and green combination of rose petal and leaf. When you want to create a dynamic color scheme with snap and style, go with a complementary color scheme. Toning down the tints with gray can produce subdued color contrasts that are still quite visually stimulating.

ANALOGOUS WITH COMPLEMENTARY ACCENTS

COMBINING ANALOGOUS COLORS WITH A COMPLEMENTARY ACCENT is called analogous with complementary accent. A closely related color scheme, the split complementary, uses the complementary colors as primary hues and an analogous color for accent.

Make a statement. Use either of these color schemes when you want to create strong visual activity. To subdue the contrast, try tints or shades instead of pure colors.

A vivid accent color need not be splattered throughout a room. In fact, it is often best to use accent colors in three or four strategic locations. Or create a single focal point by using an accent color on one object or a major design element.

THE COMPLEMENTARY COLORS in the flower motif on the plates create a pleasing and energetic color scheme. Use tints and shades to create a rich palette that provides a visually stimulating color contrast.

THE COLOR WHEEL shows all tints and shades of red and green, creating a complementary color scheme.

THE STRONG COLORS in this scheme (above) provide an agreeable combination. Orange and yellow-orange with blue-violet exemplify the analogous with complementary accent color scheme.

THE COLOR WHEEL shows all tints and shades of orange, yellow-orange, and blue-violet.

HUE (COLOR)

THE UNDILUTED COLOR from which a tint or shade is derived is referred to as its **hue**. The three primary, three secondary, and six tertiary pure colors of the color wheel (page 16) are all hues. So are the infinite number of colors that result from mixing these 12 pure hues.

As demonstrated, the color yellow has a wide range of tints and shades. Each is lighter or darker than pure yellow, but all share the same hue.

INTENSITY (PURITY)

THE PURITY OF A COLOR is referred to as its **intensity**. The most intense version of any color is the pure color, with no black or white added.

When white is added to a pure color, it diminishes the intensity by diluting the color. This is called tinting the color, and the lighter the tint, the closer it is to the center of the color wheel.

When black is added to a pure color, it produces darker, less intense derivatives of that color. This is called shading a color; the darker the shade, the farther it is toward the outside of the color wheel.

Select carefully. Many color designers prefer to stay within the same range of intensity when using different colors. In most cases, the pure color, with no black or white added, is used as an accent color.

VALUE (BRIGHTNESS)

THE BRIGHTNESS OF A COLOR, as registered by a photographer's light meter or in a black and white photograph, is its **value**.

Adding white to a color increases its value. Adding black to a color decreases its value.

A monochromatic color scheme using tints and shades of a single hue thus contains a range of values.

Colors are often described in professional circles by another set of terms: hue, intensity, and value.

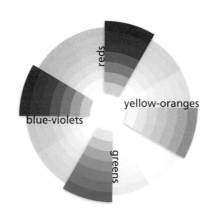

TINTS AND SHADES from the same slice of the color wheel are all the same hue.

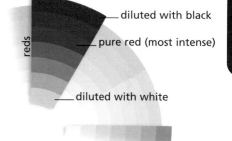

A COLOR IS MOST INTENSE in its pure form. Add white for a less intense tint; add black for a more intense shade.

HIGH VALUE   LOW VALUE

COLOR VALUES are particularly evident in black-and-white photos. High and low values create contrast and depth.

HOW LIGHT AFFECTS COLOR

The kind of light a color will be viewed under will determine how it will be perceived.

LIGHT SOURCES

COLOR IS A REFLECTION OF LIGHT. Thus the source (or type) of light plays a major role in how the eye perceives color.

Natural daylight. Daylight is known as the perfect light source because the human eye has adapted to it over thousands of years. It is characterized by having nearly uniform intensity over the entire visible spectrum of colors. (See page 15.)

The spectrum shown in the upper photograph is that of the noon sun, when atmospheric absorption is at a minimum. Near sunrise and sunset, the sun's rays have to traverse more of the atmosphere. The shorter wavelengths (blues and violets) are absorbed and scattered, shifting the spectrum toward the warmer reds.

Incandescent light. Incandescent lamps emit a greater percentage of long-wave radiation (reds) than the sun. As a result, objects they illuminate appear redder and warmer than under sunlight.

This effect is enhanced by dimmer controls. The dimmer reduces the power going to the lamp, reducing the temperature of the filament. As a result, the filament color shifts from yellow-white toward red.

Fluorescent light. Fluorescent lamps contain mercury atoms, which emit ultraviolet radiation when struck by electrons. This radiation is not visible, but it excites the phosphors coating inside of the bulb, causing it to reemit visible radiation in several peaks. One of the peaks

NATURAL DAYLIGHT

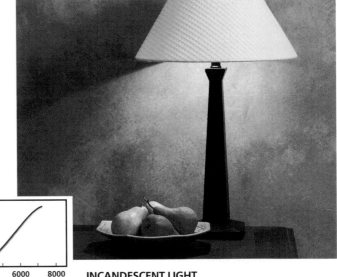

INCANDESCENT LIGHT

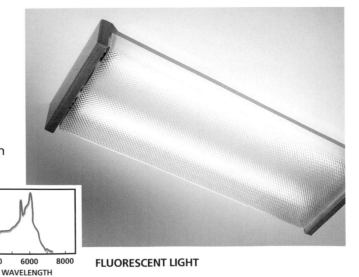

FLUORESCENT LIGHT

is near the blue end of the visible spectrum. The light from the classic cool white bulb is distinctly bluer, or cooler, than sunlight.

Manufacturers have developed mixes of phosphors that closely match natural daylight. Several bulb types are designated daylight and warm white.

EFFECTS OF THE LIGHT SOURCES

CONSIDER THE IMPACT of light on color when you make your color selections.

Natural lighting. Illuminated solely by the daylight filtering through the window, the colors in the bathroom (right) appear natural.

When selecting colors for a room that has large windows and is used predominantly during daytime hours, view samples in your home in daylight.

Incandescent lamps. Illuminated by incandescent wall lamps, the same bathroom has a warmer appearance (below).

When selecting colors, take note of the time of day a room is most often used. When you're selecting colors for a room used primarily before sunrise and after sunset, choose them under the lighting used in the room.

Fluorescent lamps. Illuminated this time by a cool white overhead fluorescent fixture, the bathroom seems cold and otherworldly (bottom).

Fluorescent light offers low-energy usage. Install lamps that more closely approximate daylight, or select warmer colors for the room. In either case, select the colors from color chips viewed under the type of lamp you plan to install.

NATURAL LIGHTING

INCANDESCENT LAMPS

FLUORESCENT LAMPS

ILLUMINATION LEVEL

THE AMOUNT OF LIGHT falling on surfaces alters our interpretation of their colors. Even though the difference in perception is one of value rather than hue, it is no less important than the effect of light sources described on page 23.

A lighter tint. Bright light falling on a surface increases the amount of light reflected back to our eye from the white component in a tint, but not from any black component. Thus, the value, or brightness, of the surface color increases in bright light. This makes objects appear more like a lighter tint.

A darker shade. Conversely, dimmer light falling on the surface decreases the white-reflected component. This decreases the intensity and value of a color, making it look like a darker shade of the same color.

When you select colors, do so with a careful eye toward the amount of light that is generally used in a room. For instance, if you want to brighten a room that has a low level of illumination, use lighter tints.

BRIGHT LIGHTING seems to lighten colors.　**DIM LIGHTING** seems to darken colors.

CLOSER LOOK

what is enamel?

IN THE PAST enamel (a porcelain finish) was sprayed on appliances to give them a rock-hard and durable finish. Now enamel on a paint usually means a finish that is durable and glossy.

CHOOSE KITCHEN COLORS when the room is used most. The amount of natural light in the room influences color perception.

CHOOSE DINING ROOM colors at night. Without natural light, the colors tend to appear darker than in daylight.

REFLECTED LIGHT SOURCE

DO YOU KNOW WHY the sea appears blue under a blue sky, but gray under a gray sky? Sea water is colorless; you see the reflection of the light illuminating it—skylight.

White surfaces reflect all colors. Thus, a painted surface with a white component (tint) will reflect some of the color of the light reflected onto it.

Floors, ceilings, even carpets and furnishings can change perceptions of the color of the wall.

WHITE WALLS with light reflecting from white carpet.

WHITE WALLS with light reflecting from red carpet.

SHEEN/FINISH (PAINT REFLECTIVITY)

SHEEN OR FINISH IS A MEASURE of the reflectivity of paint. The greater the sheen—increasing from flat through gloss—the higher the percentage of incident light reflected from the surface.

If the reflected light is white, as it would be from a white wall or ceiling, what the eye perceives is white light coming from the reflective surface.

That is why greater sheen has the same effect as greater illumination level: Sheen increases the value (brightness) of the surface.

Most paints are available in at least four of the five sheens: flat, eggshell, satin, semigloss, and gloss. Use high-gloss paint to brighten a room with little incident light; use low-gloss paint to reduce reflectivity.

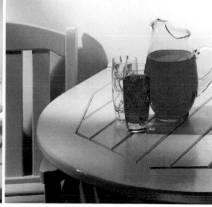

THE FIVE PAINT SHEENS, from left to right: flat, eggshell, satin, semigloss, and gloss.

FLAT PAINT reflects less light, making the color appear less bright.

GLOSS PAINT reflects more light, making the color appear brighter.

COLOR AND PERCEPTION

Take into account the impact of color on space and mood when you're creating a color scheme.

HOW COLOR AFFECTS SPACE

YOU CAN USE COLOR to alter the apparent proportions of a room.

The examples on these pages demonstrate that, for many people, dark colors make surfaces appear closer, while light colors make surfaces appear farther away.

Use contrasting colors (those that are far apart on the color wheel) to make a space appear smaller than it is. Use colors with little contrast (those that are

closer together on the color wheel) when you want to make a space appear larger than it is.

Do these effects work for you? (They don't work for everyone.) If they do, you can use color to change the perceived dimensions of your rooms without actually moving walls or ceilings.

REFERENCE ROOM

DARK WALLS make a room seem smaller.

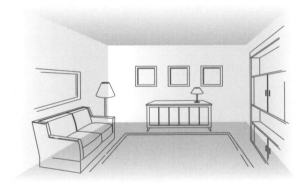

LIGHT WALLS make a room seem larger.

A DARK CEILING seems lower. Bring the ceiling color down the wall to enhance the effect of coziness.

A WHITE CEILING seems higher and makes the room feel larger and airier.

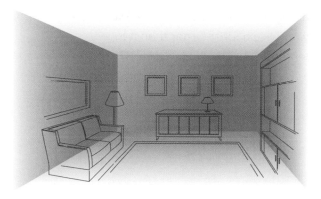

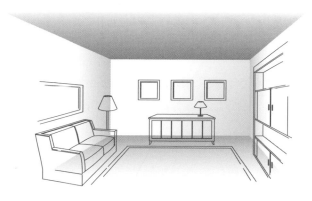

A LIGHT CEILING and dark walls may make a room appear taller and narrower.

A DARK CEILING and light walls may make a room appear shorter and wider.

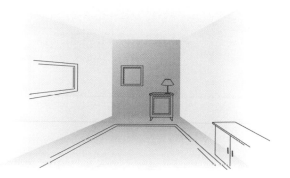

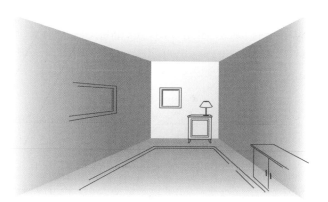

LIGHT SIDE WALLS and dark end walls may make a long hall seem shorter.

DARK SIDE WALLS and a light end wall may make a hall seem longer, but some say the effect is the opposite.

HIGH CONTRAST may appear to shrink space.

LOW CONTRAST may appear to expand space.

27

COLOR AND PERCEPTION (continued)

HOW COLOR AFFECTS OBJECTS

FOR A LESSON ON THE effect of color, look at animals in their natural surroundings. The male of many species of birds is brightly colored in order to draw the female's attention. The chameleon changes its skin color to match that of its surroundings, enabling it to visually disappear when danger is near.

You can use color to accomplish the same purpose. When you want an object to stand out, paint it a contrasting color. When you want to unify the objects in a room, paint them to match the walls.

The examples on this page demonstrate two of the ways you can use color to draw attention to a feature or to make it blend into its surroundings. As you work with color, you'll learn how to use various hues to your advantage.

TO HIGHLIGHT an object, paint it a bright, warm color, and use subdued colors around it.

TO MAKE AN OBJECT virtually disappear, paint it the same color as the walls.

MAKE DOORS and windows an element of your interior design by painting their casings contrasting colors.

DE-EMPHASIZE windows and doors by painting the casings the same color as the walls.

HOW COLOR AFFECTS OUR MOODS

HUMANS EVOLVED surrounded by the rich color palette of nature. As a result, different colors are associated with various parts of nature. And the colors of nature evoke differing moods.

For instance, cool whites and blues are associated with water, sky, and great distances; dark greens are associated with the dimly lit forest. Shades of brown feel like earth; reds remind people of warm fire.

The tint or shade of a color plays a major role in creating mood. Deep red is a passionate color; a tint of pink is more playful.

Use these associations to create the mood you desire for each space in your home. The photographs below demonstrate how colors affect mood.

WARM COLORS (those close to red on the color wheel) feel warm, energetic, and passionate.

COOL COLORS (those close to blue on the color wheel) feel cool, calm, and airy.

DARK COLORS (those shaded with the addition of black) tend to feel serious.

LIGHT COLORS (those tinted with the addition of white) tend to feel lighthearted.

COLOR MATCHING

Selecting the right hue of a color is critical to designing a scheme that works.

COLOR CHIPS

PAINT DEPARTMENTS of home centers and decorating centers typically offer thousands of color "chips" to aid in selection of a color scheme. One question the customer always asks is, "How accurate are these colors? Is this really what the paint will look like on my walls?"

Color selection tips. Paint manufacturers strive to make the chips as accurate as possible. But as with any tool, the proper use is up to you:

■ All colors look different under different light sources (see page 23). When you're choosing colors, compare several chips under the lighting conditions the room will ultimately have. Check the colors morning, noon, and night because the room lighting conditions may (and probably will) change.

■ All colored paints darken as they dry. Before you conclude that the paint you just purchased doesn't match the chip, dry a swatch with a blow dryer. They may do this for you at the store.

■ If the chips are too small, tape four or more together and hold them closer to your eye.

A COLOR CHIP rarely appears to be the same color as liquid paint in the can.

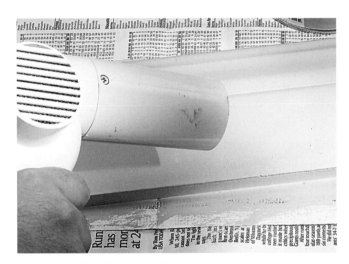

PAINT A SAMPLE BOARD and blow it dry on the no-heat setting. The result will be closer to the color you selected.

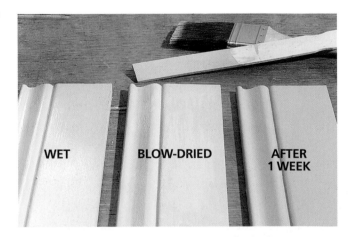

WET   BLOW-DRIED   AFTER 1 WEEK

LIQUID PAINT TENDS to look lighter than its final color. Even blow-drying the sample may not give you an accurate color match. You'll realize the final color only after the paint has cured.

COMPUTER MATCHING

WHAT IF YOU NEED to repaint only one wall of a room, and you don't have any of the old paint? Or what if you want to match the trim paint to one of the colors in a room's wallpaper?

In the past, a good painter could tint a paint on-site to match existing colors, but it required a good eye and years of experience. Today computer technology takes much of the guesswork out of color matching.

The technology edge. If you provide a clean, opaque, solid sample of the color (about the size of a quarter) that you want to match, the computer will analyze the sample and print a formula for mixing the paint.

Can you get a perfect match? If you expect the match to be close, you will usually be satisfied, but if you're looking for an exact match, you may occasionally be disappointed. The computer will also have difficulty matching colors from a piece of fabric or the pages of a magazine because the colors for printed material are created differently than they are for paint.

Note that some color chips are patented by the manufacturer, and it's illegal for the paint center to match the color.

TEST PANELS

IT'S EASIER TO PAINT TEST PANELS until you get the color you want than it is to repaint an entire room. Get quarts of the colors you're considering and paint them on 2×2-foot panels of primed drywall or foam-core panels, available at paint centers or art supply stores.

Let the panels dry for 24 hours and place them in various areas of the room you're going to decorate. View the samples under all room conditions for a full day and night. Consider surrounding colors, furniture, and works of art, as well as light sources.

 **WORK SMARTER**

stash the chips

TAPE THE COLOR CHIPS making up the color scheme for your room under the cover plate of a light switch.

COMPUTER color analyzers need only a clean, opaque, solid-color sample of paint at least the size of a quarter to do their job.

WITH THE COMPUTERIZED results, an almost exact color match can be formulated. Get two copies of the formula, tape one to the lid of the can, and keep the other in a safe place.

LOOK AT YOUR TEST PANELS in various lighting conditions. Make your final selection only after looking at each sample at different times of the day, in several different areas of the room.

TOOLS AND

MATERIALS

IN THIS SECTION: tools of the trade

EQUIPPING YOURSELF WITH THE PROPER PAINTING GEAR will save time and effort. Quality tools, well cared for, are an investment in painting success. Read on for pertinent information on how to use and care for painting gear, an overview of special tools to solve specific challenges, painting tips and techniques, and more.

A QUALITY BRUSH is worth its weight in gold and is one of the best investments a painter can make. Good brushes hold more paint, provide better coverage, and, if properly cared for, will last for generations.

THE PAINTER'S TOOL KIT

If cared for properly, quality tools will last a lifetime and will make your painting experience easier. Good tools help guarantee great results.

GOOD QUALITY TOOLS are one of the most important investments you'll make as you become more involved in home improvement projects. The tools on this page will help you get the best painting results possible. Some you may already have and some will need to be purchased. When you're preparing for a project fill out your tool list with the best products you can afford. Good tools save you time and effort.

1-QUART PAINT BUCKET
Pro recommended alternative to painting straight from the can. Inexpensive and essential.

BRUSH AND ROLLER SPINNER
Used to clean roller covers and brushes.

MIXING PADDLE
Attaches to an electric drill. Ensures even mixing of paint.

POUR SPOUT FOR GALLON CAN
Fits in the paint can's rim. Eliminates drips and spills when pouring.

ROLLERS
Applicators made of synthetic or natural fiber (of various thickness or "nap") attached to a solid core.

SPLIT FOAM ROLLER
Used for painting textured surfaces such as popcorn ceilings.

5-GALLON BUCKET
Use if applying more than one gallon on a job. Ensures even mix of color and easy storage.

BRUSHES
Quality varies, choose the right brush for the job.

PAINT CAN OPENER
Designed not to damage rim of paint can when opening.

ROLLER GRID FOR 5-GALLON BUCKET
Allows clean and even loading of paint on roller when using a 5-gallon bucket.

RUBBER SANDING BLOCK
For hand sanding. The block holds sheets of sandpaper, is easy to grip, and conforms to slightly uneven surfaces.

STAINLESS WIRE BRUSH
For removing loose paint, dirt, and rust particles.

5-IN-1 TOOL
Scraper, digger, roller cleaner, and more. Inexpensive and indispensible.

CAULKING GUN
For applying caulk to holes and cracks.

PAINTER'S TAPE
Blue (for latex) and green (for alkyd) tape formulated for easy removal.

ROLLER PAN
Holds paint that will be applied with a roller. Look for sturdy construction with a deep well.

RAGS
Indispensible for cleaning up drips and spills.

TAPE MEASURE
For measuring areas to be painted and laying out decorative patterns.

3-INCH PUTTY KNIFE
For applying and smoothing spackle. Can also be used to remove wallpaper if the corners are rounded.

EXTENSION POLE
Pole holds paint roller and telescopes to allow easy and less taxing application of paint on ceilings and high walls. Comes in several lengths.

PLASTIC MISTING BOTTLE
Used for priming (dampening slightly) roller covers and brushes before applying latex paint.

ROLLER PAN LINER
Disposable container to hold paint in roller pan Makes cleanup and multiple color use easier.

ROLLER CAGES
Buy good quality cages that will hold the roller covers securely in place while painting.

UTILITY KNIFE
For general cutting of all thin materials, such as masking tape and drop cloths. Blade alone can be used to scrape off paint drops.

BRUSH BASICS

A GOOD PAINTBRUSH feels like a natural extension of your hand. Brushes come in various qualities and prices.

Quality speaks. Bristle brushes are more expensive. They have earned their popularity with their variety of uses, ease of cleaning, and reuse capabilities. There are two types of bristles:

■ Natural (usually hog) for solvent-based finishes;

■ Synthetic (nylon or polyester) for water-based finishes. (Some can be used with oil-based finishes as well.)

The bristle edge. Compared to rollers and pads, the advantages of bristle brushes include:

■ Versatility.

■ Durability and reusability.

■ Ability to apply a heavier coat.

■ Fastest cleanup.

The other hand. The disadvantages to bristles are:

■ Slower application than a roller or pad.

■ Brush marks (a function of quality and expertise).

■ Skill required to cover large areas.

For quick projects. The least expensive are disposable brushes. They provide quick application of materials that are difficult to clean up, such as contact cement and fiberglass resin. Use low-cost foam brushes to apply smooth finishes to small areas.

Brush selection, use, and care is as critical to your success at painting as surface preparation.

TOOLS AND MATERIALS

THE RIGHT BRUSH FOR THE JOB speeds the painting process and ensures better results. A wooden handle absorbs moisture, making holding easier. A plastic handle will get slippery.

WHY QUALITY BRUSHES COST MORE

TOP QUALITY	VS.	DISPOSABLE
Flagged (split) bristle ends for a smoother finish	BRISTLES	Unflagged bristle ends
Multiple wood spacer plugs to create paint reservoirs between bristle rows	DIVIDER	Single wood spacer plug
Reinforced, rustproof ferrule to hold bristles securely	FERRULE	Weak ferrule, allowing bristles to fall out more easily
Tapered end for better control	HANDLE	Blunt point

WHAT TO LOOK FOR IN A QUALITY BRUSH

A BRISTLE LENGTH that is twice the width of the brush

A DEFINITE FLEX and snapback when pushed against your palm

ANGLED SASH BRUSHES with bristles cut at an angle to make cutting in easier and to create a softer finish

STRAIGHT, smooth bristles with no gaps hold more paint

SHEDDING no more than three or four bristles when tugged

FLAGGED (split) and tipped (varying lengths) ends for a smooth finish

DIFFERENT SHAPES FOR DIFFERENT STROKES

SASH brushes are good for reaching into corners.

SQUARE-END (flat) brushes are best for flat surfaces.

MATCH the brush width to the width of the object being painted.

Achieve stunning results by knowing how to properly use a high-quality paintbrush.

LEARN TO USE A PAINTBRUSH PROPERLY by practicing these basic techniques and using the right brush for the job. Prime (wet) the brush with the right thinner (water for latex paint, mineral spirits for alkyd) before you dip it into paint. Brush out excess thinner and load the brush with paint.

One step at a time. Painting is a three-step process: Apply a brush load, spread the paint, then smooth it to an even finish. Start the second brush load at the wet edge of the first stroke, and paint toward the dry. Then paint back toward the wet area. Feather the two areas together with light strokes. Apply a heavy coat; it will flow and hide better than if you brush the paint out too thin.

HOLD THE BRUSH handle between your thumb and forefinger, with your other fingers on the ferrule.

USE YOUR WRIST AND YOUR ARM when you paint. You'll have better control, and it's less tiring than using just your arm.

DIP THE BRISTLES only one-third of their length into the paint. This will keep paint from building up in the ferrule.

TAP BOTH SIDES OF THE LOADED BRUSH on the side of the bucket. Dragging or pressing removes too much paint.

CLOSER LOOK

bristle wise

DON'T PRESS THE BRISTLES firmly against the side of the can or bucket. Pressure will collapse and empty the reservoir between the wood spacers, as seen in this cross-sectioned brush.

QUICK TIP Don't hold the brush too tightly. Too much gripping pressure will tire your hand quickly and make painting a chore.

USING BRUSHES (continued)

1 **START YOUR FIRST BRUSH STROKE** one brush width from the end; brush away from the end.

2 **RETURN TO THE STARTING POINT** and brush toward the end. Spread, then smooth with a light touch.

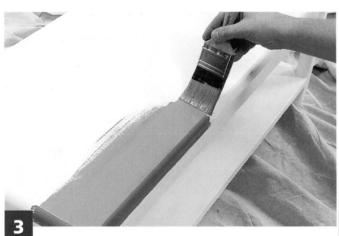

3 **TO AVOID OVERLAP MARKS,** start subsequent strokes at the wet edge of the previous stroke and paint toward dry.

4 **PAINT BACK** toward the wet area. Feather the two areas together with light strokes.

WORK SMARTER

don't overbrush

OVERBRUSHING RESULTS IN WHAT the pros call "roping," which are the lines the brush leaves in the paint because it was already partially dried when it was painted over. The general rule is, "Let it dry and fix it later."

HOMER'S HINDSIGHT

dried isn't cured

I MADE THREE MISTAKES BECAUSE I WAS IN A HURRY. I painted myself into a corner (No. 1). I got impatient because it was time for lunch (No. 2).

The paint looked dry, and felt dry to the touch, so I took a couple of giant steps toward freedom (No. 3). There's a big difference between paint that is dry to the touch and paint that has cured. (Yes, I had to paint that floor all over again, and lunch wasn't worth being in a hurry.)

PAINT ROLLERS ARE TWO-PIECE TOOLS: There is a handle with a wire cage and threaded base, and an interchangeable roller cover.

A long-term investment. The handle will last as long as you clean it, so invest in the best you can afford. Look for these features:

- A grip that molds to your hand.
- A heavy frame with minimum flex under pressure.
- Nylon bearings that spin easily.
- A cage with at least five wires and an antislip device.

For the job at hand. Roller covers range in quality. Bargain roller covers with paper cores break down quickly and cannot be reused. Use them for small jobs. Look for these features in a high-quality roller cover:

- A resin tube that won't break down in water.
- Beveled ends to avoid leaving edge beads.
- Seams that cannot be felt through the nap.
- Heavy, uniform nap that sheds little lint.

When should you use a roller? The roller lays down paint at least three times faster than the largest brush, and a good roller with beveled ends leaves no roller or overlap marks. A roller is the tool of choice for large, flat areas, such as ceilings and walls.

When should you use a brush? Use it when you need to paint narrow strips or cut in (paint a sharp edge). A roller has soft ends, so it cannot lay a sharp line of paint. For these tasks there is no substitute for a good brush.

It takes two. Most jobs will require both a roller and a paintbrush. The key is to understand when to use each applicator, and to know how to use it properly, including pouring out only as much paint as you are going to need for the job.

A paint roller offers faster and easier paint application than a brush. Select from a variety of handles and covers.

IT TAKES PRACTICE AND THE PROPER TECHNIQUES. Follow these simple steps and you'll soon be rolling paint like a pro.

THE STANDARD 9-inch roller with an extension handle is the best choice for walls and ceilings.

A 3-INCH roller is useful on flat window and door casings. The edges still have to be cut in with a brush, however.

THE FOAM "hot dog" roller lays an ultrasmooth finish on smooth, flat surfaces.

A BETTER ROLLER has a molded handle, nylon bearings, a rectangular frame of heavy wire, and a five-wire cage.

ROLLER NAPS

Use a roller cover with a long nap for rough surfaces, a short nap for smooth surfaces.

THE ROLLER NAP is the fiber that applies the paint. Select a roller nap designed for the texture of the wall you plan to paint and the type of paint you plan to use. As with everything else in life, you get what you pay for. A cheap roller has a cardboard core that quickly goes out of round and a nap that will soon come off on the surface. It costs little more to get a roller with a fiber core and well-attached nap, but it's easy to clean and will last through several jobs.

Most naps are nylon, good for both latex and alkyd paint. Lamb's wool and mohair rollers are excellent for applying alkyd paint, but they tend to soften in water-based paints and are expensive.

Common nap lengths vary from ³⁄₁₆ inch to 1¼ inches. The longer the nap fiber, the rougher the surface it will cover.

CHOOSE YOUR ROLLER NAP to match the project at hand. The smoother and glossier the surface, the shorter the nap.

USE ³⁄₁₆- AND ¼-INCH NAPS with gloss paints on smooth surfaces, such as shelving and cabinets.

USE A ³⁄₈-INCH NAP for flat and semigloss paint on walls and ceilings.

 TOOL TIP

a multipurpose tool

BUY A 5-IN-1 TOOL, if for nothing else, to use as a roller scraper. It saves paint, clears a roller of solids buildup, and speeds cleanup immensely.

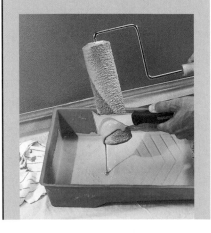

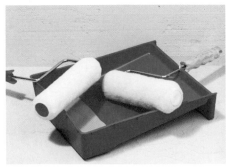

USE ½- AND ¾-INCH NAPS for semi-rough surfaces, such as concrete floors and textured walls.

USE 1- OR 1¼-INCH naps for brick, concrete block, heavy stucco, and chain-link fences.

USING A ROLLER

For speed, efficiency, and even coverage on a large space, use a paint roller.

WHEN THE CAN SAYS IT COVERS 400 SQUARE FEET it isn't kidding; most pros don't expect to get more than 300 to 350 feet. Stretching paint for extended coverage is the most common mistake beginning painters make. You'll know you've got the right amount of paint for good coverage on your roller when it doesn't slide or skip, rolls on smoothly, and doesn't drip. Let the roller do the work; use only enough pressure to get the paint on the wall.

1 **PRIME THE ROLLER** cover with a misting bottle filled with water (latex) or a rag doused in mineral spirits (alkyd) before starting. Remove excess liquid, or the first application will run.

2 **DIP THE ROLLER** cover into the tray and saturate it with paint. Then remove excess paint by gently rolling it back and forth on the grated part of the paint tray.

3 **START AT A CORNER** (your choice), and make your first application a giant 3×3-foot W pattern. If the paint drips, start with an upstroke, making an M.

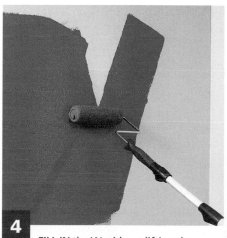

4 **FILL IN** the W without lifting the roller. If the roller begins to "talk" it is too dry; try smaller Ws. Continue down and across, blending sections together.

5 **BACK-ROLL FROM FLOOR TO CEILING.** Fill the roller with a light load of paint and back-roll the sections you've finished to smooth out the finish and remove race tracks, lap marks, drips, and bare spots.

TIME SAVER

power up

A POWER ROLLER SPEEDS PAINTING and reduces cleanup. Paint is fed to the roller via a tube attached to  a pump that is immersed in the paint can. Just press the handle trigger to reload the roller with fresh paint.

OTHER APPLICATORS

Special challenges demand specific tools. Here's the scoop on applicators to get you out of tight corners.

PAINT CENTERS OFFER various special-purpose paint applicators, each designed to solve a specific problem that brushes and rollers can't deal with. Except for the paint sprayer, these tools are inexpensive and will, more than likely, pay for themselves in a single job.

Quite frankly, the expense of a good paint sprayer is minimal in comparison to the time it can save when you're painting uneven or rough surfaces.

Before you head to the store, assess the challenges of the project at hand. Are there tight corners, narrow strips, or uneven surfaces? Does your project include spindles, balusters, or pipes? Will you mask off all borders? Special applicators help simplify such tasks.

Ask the experts. If you have other difficult applications, ask the store associates at The Home Depot for help. They will offer sound painting tips, provide good advice for difficult techniques, and lead you to the right tool for the job.

AN AIRLESS SPRAYER is the fastest way to apply paint to an uneven surface, such as this wainscoting, but requires straining, a lot of masking, and the most cleanup. Back-roll after spraying for best results.

A PAINT PAD applies an extremely smooth layer of paint, but it holds little paint. It's an excellent choice for creating smooth finishes on small areas, however.

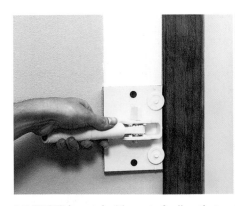

AN EDGER is a pad with a set of rollers that keep the pad from touching the adjacent surface. In some cases it can save you from masking a border.

THE CORNER PAD is a special-purpose tool for cutting in room corners. Do one room corner at a time so you can blend the edges while the paint is wet.

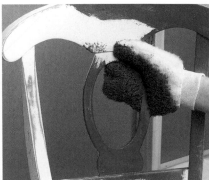

A PAINT MITT, dipped in a paint tray, makes fast work of spindles, balusters, wrought iron, and pipes. Buy some extra mitts—kids get a kick out of helping.

PAINT ALWAYS ENDS UP where you don't want it. You can stop and clean as you go, or you can protect vulnerable surfaces before you start, saving you time in the long run. Remove the furniture, if possible, and protect floors, windows, doors, trim and baseboards, and light fixtures. Protect yourself with an old long-sleeved shirt and pants—or purchase painter's coveralls and hoods.

Spatter-proof the room. To protect large surfaces and furnishings, invest in a good drop cloth. You will generally find three types:
1. Polyethylene sheeting (poly) is inexpensive but slippery (see buyer's guide below).
2. Canvas is the toughest and most expensive, but it can leak water-based (latex) paints.
3. Paper/poly (fuzzy paper on one side and plastic on the other) is waterproof, less slippery than poly, and less expensive than canvas. It's a good solution for interior projects.

To protect trim and other margins, use blue painter's tape—a low-residue masking tape that won't mar or damage finished surfaces when you remove it.

PROTECTING OTHER SURFACES

Good prep means a faster, neater, and more successful job. Protecting surrounding surfaces is essential.

A PAINTER'S CAP keeps the spatters out of your hair when you're painting overhead.

A PAINTER'S COVERALL offers neck-to-toe protection and "breathes" to keep you cool.

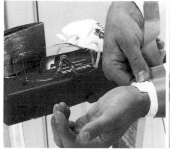

WHEN SANDING or spray painting, cinch your sleeves and cuffs with masking tape.

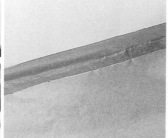

BLUE PAINTER'S TAPE can remain for up to a week while prepping but must be removed immediately after painting.

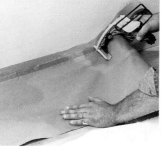

PAPER masking combined with self-adhesive blue painter's tape is perfect for protecting baseboards and trim. Various widths are available.

SLIP A PAPER/POLY drop cloth under the baseboard masking for complete floor protection.

BUYER'S GUIDE

1 POLY SHEETING, the least expensive, is waterproof but slippery underfoot.

2 CANVAS will last longest but is not waterproof; water-based (latex) paints will probably soak through it.

3 PAPER/POLY is a good compromise. It is waterproof and less slippery than poly sheeting.

STEPLADDERS

Safety, convenience, and comfort: That's how a good stepladder pays for itself.

A GOOD STEPLADDER provides the stability you need to paint out-of-reach areas. For ceilings 8 feet or lower, a 4-foot stepladder is adequate; in homes with higher ceilings, you'll need at least a 6-foot stepladder. Price is based on the materials used in the ladder's construction.

■ Though expensive, fiberglass ladders are lightweight, strong, and do not conduct electricity.

■ Aluminum is nearly as lightweight and strong, and about half the price of fiberglass.

■ Wood is heaviest and the least expensive.

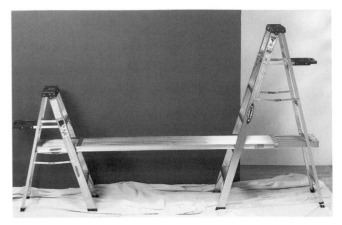

USE TWO LADDERS AND A PLANK to build a scaffold that is safe, convenient, and relatively easy to move. Snap the ladder's locking bars in place and set the plank on the steps. Never use the fold-out shelf as a step.

When you're shopping for a ladder, look for special features to make your job easier. For instance, some foldout shelves include a paper towel holder, tracks for hand tools, even a special paint bucket holder.

Regardless of the kind or size of ladder, follow the safety rules illustrated on this page.

NEVER EXCEED the manufacturer's weight rating printed on the yellow sticker. And don't remove the sticker!

MAKE SURE the locking bars are snapped in the locked position before setting in place and using the ladder.

USE THE FOLDOUT SHELF to hold your bucket or roller tray—not as a step. Don't even stand on the step opposite the shelf.

WORK SAFELY

NEVER STAND on the top step of a ladder—not even just this once or for just a moment. Use a taller ladder if necessary to reach the highest points.

TO PAINT ABOVE a stairway, set a tall stepladder on the bottom stair landing and run a plank from a stair tread to the ladder step that is closest to the same level. Firmly position the plank between the step and the ladder; wear slip-resistant shoes. Maintain your balance, and don't stand on the edge of the plank.

YOU ARE VULNERABLE to particles and fumes when you are sanding, painting, or working with solvents.

To protect your skin:

■ Wear cotton gloves when using sharp or abrasive tools.

■ Wear latex gloves when painting with latex paint.

NEOPRENE GLOVES

■ Wear neoprene gloves when handling solvents, strippers, and harsh chemicals.

To protect your eyes:

■ Wear safety glasses when working with tools.

SAFETY GOGGLES

■ Wear goggles to protect against dust and aerosol droplets when sanding, spraying, or painting over your head.

To protect your lungs:

■ Sand, paint, and strip outside, or cross-ventilate with at least two open windows or doors.

■ If there is a danger of breathing dust, aerosols, or solvent fumes, filter the air with a respirator. Check product labels for the recommended respirator.

RESPIRATORS are of two types:

Particulate respirators (dust-resistant masks) filter out dry particles and most non-oil-based liquid droplets. Use a particulate respirator when sanding bare or painted wood (except lead-based paint), drywall, and rusted surfaces. Special-purpose particulate respirators are available for spraying latex paint and sanding (not burning) lead-based paint.

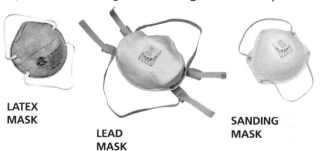

LATEX MASK

LEAD MASK

SANDING MASK

SAFETY EQUIPMENT

Follow these tips to work safely. It's the most important part of any home improvement project.

Cartridge respirators contain both particulate filters and chemically active canisters for absorbing solvent vapors. Use a cartridge respirator when spraying solvent-based paints and working with solvents and strippers.

Note: Unless specifically stated otherwise, no homeowner-type respirator protects against lead fumes, asbestos fibers, or sandblasting.

CARTRIDGE RESPIRATOR

Fitting respirators. A respirator must form an airtight seal around nose and mouth. Respirators don't work with beards. To fit a particulate respirator:

■ Position the mask under your chin.

■ Pull the top and bottom straps over your head and position them just above and below your ears.

■ Using the same fingers of both hands, mold the soft metal nose strap to your nose.

■ Test the fit by covering the mask with both hands and drawing a sharp breath; it should be difficult to breathe.

To fit a cartridge respirator:

■ Place the respirator loosely over your face, low on the bridge of your nose.

■ Fasten the straps for a snug but comfortable fit.

■ Test the fit by covering the air inlets and breathing out gently. The mask should bulge slightly, and you should neither hear nor feel any leakage. If you smell fumes or feel dizzy, either the respirator doesn't fit, the canisters are the wrong type, or they are used up.

Always read the warnings on paint, solvent, and stripper containers, and compare them to the listed capabilities of the respirator canister.

3

PREPARING TO PAINT

IN THIS SECTION: preparation basics

PREPARATION TREMENDOUSLY INFLUENCES THE FINAL RESULT. A paint job is only as good as the time that went in to getting the surfaces smooth, clean, and primed. No matter how expensive the paint, it won't hide mistakes. You'll actually save time later by taking the time now to prepare the surfaces you're going to paint.

CAREFULLY MASKING THE TRIM AND WOODWORK allows you to concentrate on getting paint on the walls without worrying about the inevitable spatters and spills.

REMOVING WALLPAPER

To save time and protect plaster or drywall from scrapes, perforate and spray wallpaper before you rip it off.

STUFF YOU'LL NEED

TOOLS: Screwdriver, wallpaper perforating tool, spray bottle or garden sprayer, rubber gloves, sponge, 3-inch plastic or metal scraper

MATERIALS: 12-inch baseboard masking, blue painter's masking tape, paper/poly drop cloth, wallpaper remover (white vinegar or a chemical remover)

THE KEYS TO REMOVING WALLPAPER are patience and procedure.

Don't just start ripping off wallpaper, even if it has lifted in places. Wallpaper is applied with adhesive. Unless that adhesive is softened, you'll peel off some of the underlying drywall face paper with the wallpaper. That adds another repair process to the project.

Perforate and moisturize. First, perforate the wallpaper with hundreds of small holes. The wallpaper remover will seep through these holes and dissolve the adhesive. Next, spray the wallpaper with a softening chemical. You can use a solution of white vinegar or a chemical remover.

Here's how it works: Spray wallpaper with remover, move to a dry area, spray it, return to the first area, and spray again. Given time, holes, and several wettings, wallpaper will come off. You must give the remover time to work. Test a small corner after it has soaked for 20 minutes. If the paper doesn't come off easily, apply more remover.

CLOSER LOOK

removing wallpaper from unprimed drywall

THERE SHOULD BE A LAW AGAINST PUTTING WALLPAPER OVER UNPRIMED DRYWALL. But since there isn't, you can try removing a test section with wallpaper remover. If the top layer of drywall comes off with the wallpaper, you'll probably have to prime and paint over the wallpaper.

1 TURN OFF THE POWER AT THE CIRCUIT BREAKER PANEL. Plug a radio into the outlet and turn on any lights in the room controlled by wall switches. Then switch off circuit breakers until both the radio and the lights go off.

2 REMOVE ALL SWITCH and outlet covers on the wall you are stripping by removing the visible screws. Cover switches and outlets with blue painter's masking tape.

WORK SMARTER

how many layers

BEFORE REMOVING WALLPAPER, determine the number of layers. To investigate without causing visible damage, remove an outlet cover plate. You can lift the edges of the layers with a utility knife or razor blade and find out what you're getting into without marring the wall.

3   **COVER THE FLOOR** with a moisture-proof drop cloth, then apply 12-inch baseboard masking and blue painter's masking tape to the baseboards. Allow it to overlap the drop cloth for complete coverage.

4   **PERFORATE THE WALLPAPER** for water penetration. A "paper tiger" perforation tool is fast and effective. Don't press too hard or you'll damage the underlying drywall.

BUYER'S GUIDE

break tradition

TRADITIONAL CANVAS DROP CLOTHS are heavy and expensive, and they are not

the best choice for water or water-based paint spills which soak right through the canvas. Use a paper/poly drop cloth instead.

5   **APPLY WALLPAPER REMOVER** to an entire wall with a spray bottle or garden sprayer. Both are available at garden shops. Mix the remover with hot water to speed removal.

6   **WAIT 10 TO 20 MINUTES.** Then, wearing rubber gloves, peel off as much wallpaper as you can with your hands. Before turning to the scraper, spray on a second application of remover.

REMOVING WALLPAPER (continued)

PREPARING TO PAINT

7   **PEEL OFF REMAINING WALLPAPER** with a plastic scraper or a 3-inch putty knife. Don't damage the drywall or you'll have to repair the surface.

8   **AFTER REMOVING ALL OF THE WALLPAPER,** wash the wall several times using fresh water and a sponge to remove paste residue. Any remaining residue will reduce bonding of the paint.

REMOVING NONPAPER WALLCOVERINGS

OF ALL WALLPAPER TYPES, vinyl is the smoothest to remove because it doesn't tear easily. However, it is waterproof, so you must perforate its surface extensively to soften the underlying adhesive.

GRASS CLOTH IS MOST DIFFICULT TO REMOVE because it falls apart, leaving a real mess of grass and paste. If you encounter grass cloth or foil, you may want to call a professional.

CLOSER LOOK

round the edges

IF YOU USE A METAL SCRAPER or putty knife to remove wallpaper, file or sand the corners round. This will reduce the chance of gouging or scraping the paper face of the drywall.

QUICK TIP   Wet the wallpaper thoroughly with water as hot as you can stand. It will make removal much easier.

PAINTING OVER WALLPAPER

Sometimes it's difficult to remove the old wallpaper, but with proper preparation you can paint over it.

IF THE WALLPAPER IS SECURELY ATTACHED TO THE WALL and the seams don't show, it's often easier to paint over wallpaper rather than remove it. Once again, the finished job will only be as good as the preparation you put into it.

WORK SMARTER

fix damaged drywall

IF THE DRYWALL wasn't primed before it was papered, you probably won't be able to avoid pulling some of the drywall paper off with the wallpaper.

Small areas of damage can be smoothed with joint compound. If the damage is extensive, paper the wall with horizontal strips of wallpaper liner or apply new drywall.

1 **RESIDUAL WALLPAPER PASTE** is invisible and interferes with paint adhesion. To remove it, wipe the wall thoroughly with a wet sponge.

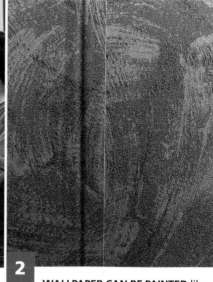

2 **WALLPAPER CAN BE PAINTED** like drywall, but overlapping and open seams will show. In that case, remove the paper or prime the wall and smooth the wall with a thin coat of joint compound.

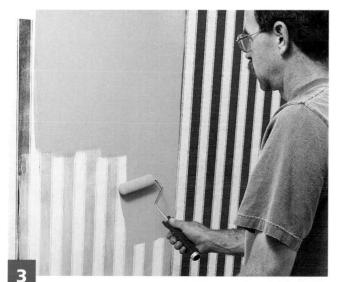

3 **ON A TEST AREA, APPLY A TINTED SHELLAC-BASED STAIN-BLOCKING PRIMER.** Wait 24 hours. Repair minor blisters or bubbles by cutting a slit with a utility knife and gluing the paper to the wall. Apply the finish coat. If the coverage looks good, finish priming and painting.

CLOSE LOOK

stain blockers

WHEN THE WALLPAPER IS DRY, a stain-blocking primer may continue to reveal the problem you're trying to make go away. In fact, it's doing its job, which is just blocking the stain. Test with your finish color to see if the blocker is effective.

STRIPPING WOOD

Strip cracked and peeling paint from wood surfaces to prepare them for a fresh coat of paint.

STUFF YOU'LL NEED

TOOLS: Screwdriver, hammer, pair of sawhorses, disposable brush, brass-wire brush, wide putty knife, neoprene rubber gloves, safety goggles, vapor respirator

MATERIALS: 1 quart of liquid paint stripper, mineral spirits (for petroleum distillate-based stripper), clean rags,

HOW YOU STRIP FINISH from wood depends on what you are removing. Most paints and clear finishes can be removed with off-the-shelf stripper.

For your convenience. Stripper is available as liquid and semi-paste. Use the easier liquid form for horizontal surfaces. Remove doors from their hinges and suspend them on sawhorses (see "Painting Doors," page 89). Use the paste form to strip vertical surfaces where liquid stripper won't stay put.

If there are multiple coats, suspect lead-based paint. Remove the first layers with a semi-paste stripper, then test remaining paint with a lead test kit. If the paint is lead based, do not sand the surface until all traces of paint have been removed with stripper.

Work in a well-ventilated space. Wear solvent-resistant rubber gloves, safety goggles, and a mask or respirator as recommended by the manufacturer. Take frequent breaks for fresh air. Keep children and pets out of the area.

BUYER'S GUIDE

make an informed selection

THERE ARE TWO CHEMICAL formulations of stripper: water based and solvent based.

Use a water-based stripper whenever you can because it:
- Emits fewer fumes.
- Washes up with water.
- Won't attack plastic surfaces.

Use a solvent-based stripper if the water in a water-based stripper would cause harmful swelling of the wood.

Both water- and solvent-based strippers require neutralization or the residual may be reactivated by the liquid in the paint. Follow the manufacturer's instructions for cleanup before painting.

WORK SMARTER

protect those floors

STRIPPER ISN'T SELECTIVE in what it strips. Cover the floor with a drop cloth so the stripper won't leak through. Wood floors will take a beating but vinyl floors will be ruined.

safety first

CHEMICAL STRIPPERS and oil-based paints can be toxic. Work safely!
- Make sure there is good ventilation; open all of the windows and use fans, or take the project outdoors.
- To dispose of old paint, put it in a metal can to dry. When it's completely dry, put it in the trash. For lead-based paint, check with local authorities.
- When using volatile oil-based paint, extinguish all pilot lights and halogen lamps, which are as hot as a flame.

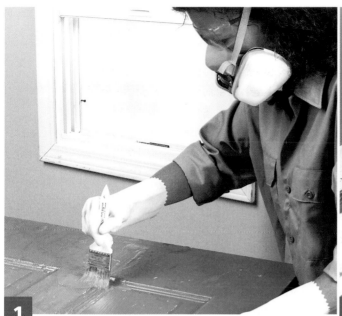

1 APPLY A HEAVY COAT OF LIQUID STRIPPER with a disposable brush. Spread the solvent without brushing it into the surface. Leave the solvent undisturbed for the recommended amount of time. Wear the type of respirator recommended by the solvent manufacturer.

2 SCRAPE OFF THE SOFTENED PAINT and stripper with a wide-blade metal putty knife. Sand or file the knife's corners round to avoid marring the wood.

3 REMOVE PAINT and stripper from intricate surfaces with a brass-wire brush. Brass bristles are softer than steel and are less likely to scratch the wood. Synthetic fiber brushes are also available.

4 UNLESS THERE IS ONLY ONE COAT of paint, you will probably not get it all on the first try. Repeat the application of stripper as many times as you need.

5 WASH OFF THE PAINT and stripper residue using a rag and either mineral spirits or water. Read the manufacturer's instructions on the label to see which is recommended.

WORK SMARTER

don't overbrush

STRIPPERS WORK BEST when applied in a thick coat and brushed on in one stroke and in one direction. Why? The top layer forms a protective coating, allowing the stripper underneath to activate and do its job. If the top layer is disturbed, the solution underneath begins to dry.

USING A HEAT GUN

A HEAT GUN IS ANOTHER OPTION for removing paint. But beware: Unless used with great care, a heat gun reduces paint to a gooey mess. Overheating the paint will produce noxious fumes. If the heat gun is too close to the surface or moved too slowly, you'll ignite a flame, burning the paint and the underlying wood. Flaming paint leaves black soot on adjacent surfaces; burning the wood makes it necessary to sand deeply to prepare the wood for a stain or clear finish.

Scrape melted paint from grooves and indentations first. Leave melted paint on higher areas to protect the underlying wood from burning.

Wear a respirator and rubber gloves.

watch what you inhale

LEAD-BASED PAINT FUMES are toxic. Before using a heat gun on paint that may be older than 1978, test it for lead. Test kits are available at home centers and paint stores. For further guidance, contact the EPA at 1-800-424LEAD or www.epa.gov.

WORK SMARTER

heat guns are hot

THE END OF A HEAT GUN is hot enough to cause severe burns. Be aware and be careful!

ALTHOUGH SIMILAR in appearance to a blow-dryer, a heat gun generates a much higher air temperature and is ideal for softening paint for removal.

KEEP THE HEAT GUN MOVING. Its discharge is hot enough to burn the paint and, if you are not careful, can ignite the wood beneath. Keep a misting bottle handy to cool things off, and remember that the tip is extremely hot.

THE GOAL is to soften the paint enough that it can be scraped off. You will know when the paint is soft enough by the small bubbles.

AS SOON AS THE BUBBLES APPEAR, scrape the softened paint off with a putty knife. If you wait too long, the paint will harden and you will have to reheat it.

HARDWARE
AND KNOBS

ALL IT TAKES IS A TRIP TO THE HARDWARE STORE to realize that it's worth your time to save those old knobs and hardware on your cabinets. Also, it's often difficult, if not impossible, to find exact replacements for real antiques. It's easy to strip paint from knobs, hinges, and other hardware when you remove them to repaint cabinets and drawers.

1 **PAINTING CABINET** and drawer fronts is simpler if you first remove the knobs. Most are attached with machine screws on the inside of the door or drawer.

2 **TO REMOVE PAINT** from these fittings, simply place them in a container of paint stripper overnight.

3 **THE FINISHED PRODUCT AFTER RINSING AND WIPING.** Wear rubber gloves to wipe off the stripper and paint, and rinse the fittings following instructions on the container. The stripper can be reused.

REDOING A BRASS FINISH

THE LACQUER USED to preserve brass is not a permanent finish. Over the years, this thin, protective coating yellows, cracks, and peels.

To recapture the deep sheen of highly polished brass, remove the lacquer, polish the metal, and reapply a protective coat.

Thinner is toxic and flammable. Think safety and wear rubber gloves, work in adequate ventilation wearing an appropriate respirator, and extinguish open flames. Don't use wax or brass polish on a lacquered finish; polish it with a soft cloth.

1 **UNPROTECTED BRASS** tarnishes quickly, so it is often coated with clear lacquer. To refurbish the brass, remove the old lacquer with lacquer thinner and a rag.

2 **AFTER ALL** of the old lacquer has been removed, use brass cleaner to remove tarnish and polish the brass. Never use wax on brass; use brass polish.

3 **WHEN THE BRASS** is as shiny as it can be, spray it with lacquer. Two thin coats are better than one thick application. Protect surrounding surfaces.

PLASTER
REPAIRS

Repairs to a plaster wall take time, patience, and know-how. The results are well worth the effort.

PLASTER BASICS

REPAIRING PLASTER IS NO MORE difficult than repairing drywall.

Plaster is applied in three thin layers over lath. Originally, lath was made of thin wooden strips nailed to the studs in the wall; now it is constructed of expanded metal or gypsum.

Start at the source. Fix whatever is causing the larger problem first:

■ Cracks are often the sign of a house settling. If you can't find the cause of the movement, call a home inspector to help.

■ Brown spots or crumbled plaster signal water damage. The roof or a water pipe may have leaked. A bathtub, toilet, or washing machine may have overflowed. Fix the water problem before repairing the plaster.

It is difficult to tell how far plaster damage extends. You have to remove all the loose material in order to get a good repair. Keep chipping away until you reach the point where the plaster is securely attached to the wall. That will give you the scope of the repair. In some cases so much plaster will come off that it's easier to complete the demolition and put up drywall in its place.

WORK SMARTER

assemble the right stuff

WHEN REPAIRING HOLES, have all the tools and materials in place before you begin.

GOOD IDEA

fix it first

Before repairing a hole or dent in plaster or drywall where a doorknob hit the wall, fix the cause.

Screw a doorstop into the baseboard below the wall. This will stop the door before the knob hits the wall. Hinge-mounted stops are also available.

BUYER'S GUIDE

plaster repair materials

Lightweight spackling compound is used for filling nail holes and hairline cracks. It is easily sanded, and dries in 15 to 30 minutes.

Patching plaster, which is mixed from powder, is for filling larger holes and cracks up to ¼ inch wide. It is applied in layers of ¼ inch maximum thickness. It is sandable, and dries in 90 minutes.

Plaster of Paris is mixed from powder and water. It is extremely durable but difficult to sand. A ¼ inch thickness hardens in 30 minutes.

Paintable latex caulk is the only filler that can handle unstable gaps and cracks in a wall or ceiling. It can be painted, but not sanded. Smooth it immediately after application.

PATCHING A PLASTER CRACK

THE DIFFERENCE IN PATCHING PLASTER and drywall is a matter of depth. With drywall, once you've eliminated the torn paper surface, you're ready to repair. With plaster, the damage goes deeper.

It's critical to remove all damaged plaster. Attaching repair materials to an unsound base is the start of a new mess: The new material will crack and peel, and can cause even more damage than the original mar.

It is equally important to allow plaster repair to dry thoroughly. The thicker the coat, the longer it will take to dry. If it's too thick, the plaster repair will crack. It is better to apply several thin coats of plaster repair than one thick coat.

1 **UNDERCUT THE CRACK.** Use a 5-in-1 tool to make the crack wider beneath the surface of the wall than it is on the surface itself. Think of an inverted V in the wall.

2 **BLOW OUT** the loose debris, then fill the undercut crack with lightweight crack filler.

3 **ALLOW THE FILLER TO DRY FOR** 24 hours, then sand the repair lightly using a sanding block with 220-grit sandpaper.

4 **PRIME THE REPAIRED AREA** with a latex, stain-blocking primer. Allow the primer to dry thoroughly before you apply the final coat over the repair. Prime the entire wall if you're changing the color.

BUYER'S GUIDE

special recipe for wider cracks

IF THE CRACK is more than ¼ inch wide, mix equal amounts of fast-drying plaster repair and dry joint compound. The resulting mix has strength and durability, can be sanded as easily as joint compound, and sets quickly.

PLASTER REPAIRS (continued)

PATCHING A HOLE IN PLASTER
A HOLE IN A PLASTER WALL IS EASY TO FIX.

However, you have to work carefully so you don't create more damage.

Unfortunately, all damaged and crumbling plaster must be removed no matter how big the repair becomes. Since you'll be plugging the hole with a piece of drywall, you'll need to cut a square opening.

Further, it's important to clean the wall around the hole because you'll be plastering, sanding, and painting there. If the wall is not clean, the paint won't adhere.

Finally, remember that plaster repair is dusty. If it's a big job, protect the surrounding area with drop cloths and mask off entrances.

1 **USING A SMALL SQUARE,** pencil a rectangular outline at least 2 inches back from the damaged area.

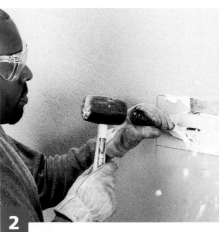

2 **CAREFULLY AND GENTLY** remove the plaster inside the rectangle down to the wooden lath using a sharp chisel and a mallet. Plaster cracks easily, so be careful!

3 **MEASURE THE DEPTH** of the plaster to the wooden lath with a tape measure.

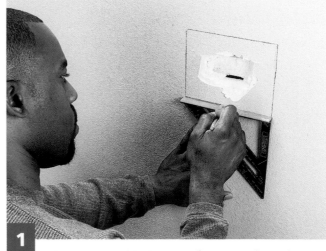

4 **USING DRYWALL** that is thinner than the plaster depth, cut a piece at least 2 inches larger than the repair hole on all sides.

5 **TRIM THE GYPSUM CORE** material back to the size of the rectangular hole it will fill.

6 **THE RESULT** is a gypsum plug with a 2-inch paper flap on all sides.

7 **SPREAD A THIN,** 3-inch-wide layer of joint compound on the perimeter of the hole.

8 **APPLY ADDITIONAL** joint compound to the back side of the drywall plug.

9 **PRESS THE PLUG** into the hole until it is flush with the wall. Squeeze out excess compound with a putty knife.

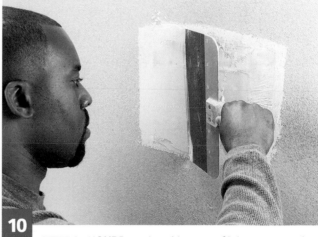

10 **AFTER 24 HOURS,** apply a skim coat of joint compound over the patch and feather the edges using a 12-inch joint knife.

11 **AFTER A SECOND 24 HOURS,** smooth the area using a sanding block with 220-grit sandpaper.

12 **SPOT PRIME THE AREA** with latex, stain-blocking primer, then repaint the wall. For maximum uniformity, prime the entire wall before you proceed.

DRYWALL REPAIRS

Learn these few simple techniques and you'll soon be repairing drywall like a pro.

NAIL HOLES AND DENTS

DRYWALL IS SOFTER than plaster, making it more vulnerable to dents and dings than a plaster wall. Consequently, there will be more repairs.

The repairs, however, are relatively simple. Just keep a small tub of joint compound and a putty knife in your tool kit—and have patience. Drywall repairs need to dry thoroughly before you paint over them.

STUFF YOU'LL NEED

TOOLS: 3- and 6-inch drywall knives, phillips screwdriver, sanding block

MATERIALS: 220-grit sandpaper, drywall joint compound, PVA drywall primer, self-adhesive wallboard patch

1 **FILL THE HOLE** or dent with drywall joint compound using a 3-inch drywall knife. If the dent is deep, apply a second coat after 24 hours.

2 **AFTER 24 HOURS,** sand the spot smooth using a sanding block with 220-grit sandpaper. Apply light pressure so you don't roughen the paper wallboard face.

NAIL POPS

WHEN DRYWALL is installed over unseasoned wood framing or strapping, the wood shrinks. The nails or screws that secure the drywall to the frame don't shrink with the wood, however. They just project out farther than when installed.

The first time the drywall is pushed against the wood, the fastener pops out of the surface. These "pops" are relatively easy to repair. And the repair is permanent unless the wood gets wet again.

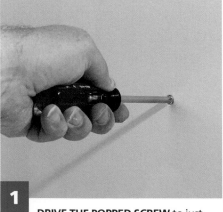

1 **DRIVE THE POPPED SCREW** to just below the wall surface. (If it's a nail, set it). Be careful not to puncture the paper face of the drywall.

2 **COVER THE HEAD** with a skim coat of drywall compound. After 24 hours, sand smooth with 220-grit paper, then spot prime the repair.

PATCHING SMALL HOLES

THESE DAYS, METAL OR FIBERGLASS patch kits simplify the repair of small holes in drywall.

Before patches were available, even a small repair required that backing material be stuffed into the hole. It would serve as a stop for the repair compound. If the hole led to a stud cavity, filling it was problematic.

With a repair kit, you simply cut the self-adhesive patch to fit. A skim coat of joint compound will attach the patch to the wall over the hole. The patch becomes embedded in the joint compound and serves to hold it in place, as well as reinforce it.

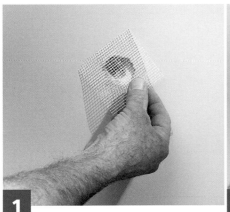

1 **CUT AND APPLY** a piece of self-adhesive wallboard patch, overlapping the hole by 1 inch on all sides.

2 **APPLY JOINT** compound over the patch using a 6-inch drywall knife.

3 **AFTER THE COMPOUND DRIES,** sand smooth using a sanding block with 220-grit sandpaper. Spot prime the repair.

REPAIRING CORNER BEAD

CORNER BEAD IS PERFORATED metal that is angle-nailed over drywall on outside corners. This raises the corner and serves to protect the drywall against blows.

A major collision can leave an indentation. Pulling the metal bead back into shape is not possible without redoing the corner completely, but careful filling of the dent with drywall compound, using a wide drywall knife, can restore the appearance of the corner.

1 **USE A PAINT SCRAPER** or utility knife to remove all of the loose and damaged drywall compound from the metal corner bead.

2 **REFILL THE DAMAGED AREA** with drywall compound, using either a 6-inch drywall knife or a drywall corner tool.

3 **AFTER THE COMPOUND DRIES,** sand the repaired area using a sanding block with 220-grit sandpaper. Prime the repair with stain-blocking primer.

DRYWALL REPAIRS (continued)

PATCHING A LARGE HOLE

AT FIRST SIGHT a large hole punched through drywall looks like a major repair job. In fact, it takes just a few hours of work, spread over a day or two.

Drywall repairs generate dust. While you're sanding, protect your eyes with safety goggles and wear a mask to avoid inhaling dust.

STUFF YOU'LL NEED

TOOLS: Framing square, pencil, keyhole saw, utility knife, phillips screwdriver, wood saw, 3-, 6-, and 12-inch drywall knives, sanding block

MATERIALS: ⅜- or ½-inch drywall, drywall screws, small piece of lumber or ½-inch plywood, drywall joint compound, paper or fiberglass joint tape, drywall primer, 220-grit sandpaper

DON'T LIVE WITH IT: Fix it! A hole in the wall is not as major a repair as it looks.

BUYER'S GUIDE — drywall repair materials

Lightweight spackling compound is used for shallow dents and nail holes. It is easily sanded, and dries in 15 to 30 minutes.

Spackling paste is for filling larger holes and dents. It must be built up in layers of ¼ inch thickness. It dries in 10 to 40 minutes and is sandable.

Wallboard joint compound is strictly for covering taped wallboard joints. It must be applied in thicknesses no greater than ¼ inch. Available in up to 5-gallon containers, it is easily sanded.

Paintable latex caulk is the only filler that can handle unstable gaps and cracks on surfaces. It can be painted, but it cannot be sanded. Smooth immediately after application.

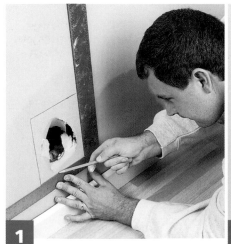

1 **USING A SQUARE** and pencil, draw a rectangle around the edges of the hole.

2 **START THE HOLE** with a keyhole saw. Use a utility knife to puncture the drywall paper if necessary.

3 **SAW AROUND** all four sides of the rectangle. Remove the damaged drywall.

PREPARING TO PAINT

4 **CUT A STRIP** of wood several inches longer than the hole. Slide it behind the drywall and fasten it with drywall screws.

5 **CUT OUT** a rectangular plug of drywall of the same thickness as that in the wall. Make it 1⁄8 inch smaller than the hole in both dimensions.

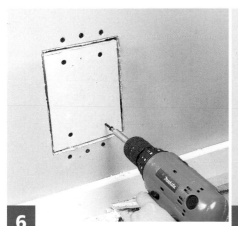

6 **PLACE THE DRYWALL PLUG** against the wood backer in the hole and screw it to the wood using drywall screws.

7 **APPLY JOINT COMPOUND** to the perimeter of the plug. Then embed paper or fiberglass joint tape in the wet compound with a 3-inch drywall knife.

8 **AFTER 24 HOURS** sand the high spots, then cover the taped area with joint compound, using a 6-inch drywall knife.

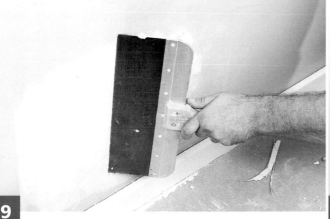

9 **AFTER A SECOND 24 HOURS,** sand lightly. Apply a final layer of compound with a 12-inch drywall knife. Feather the edges smooth.

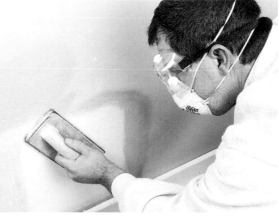

10 **SAND THE ENTIRE AREA** smooth using a drywall sanding block with 220-grit sandpaper. Prime the area with latex, stain-blocking primer before painting.

TEXTURED WALLS

Clean the walls thoroughly, or fresh paint will peel where there is grime and every stain will bleed through.

TEXTURED FINISHES are popular for covering drywall without the usual labor-intensive, three-coat taping. Application is simple, but repair can be tricky.

TEXTURE TYPES.

Sand-texture paint is interior latex paint applied by roller, containing perlite, a sandlike additive, available in fine, medium, and coarse particle sizes. The additive can be purchased separately, or premixed in 1- and 5-gallon sizes.

Orange peel is a slightly pebbly finish without the sharpness of sand. It is applied, after priming, with a spray gun, and covered with white-pigmented shellac primer and a satin or semigloss top coat. It is a good choice for both bath and kitchen because it is durable and scrubbable.

Knockdown is a two-step process. A rough, ⅛-inch coating is sprayed on, followed 10 to 15 minutes later by a second person "knocking down" the high points with a mason's trowel. The result is a hand-plastered, old-world look, popular in living rooms, bedrooms, and hallways.

Acoustic (also known as popcorn) is used on ceilings. It can be applied with a looped texture roller, or sprayed on.

APPLICATION TOOLS.

Sand-texture paint is applied with a thick-napped roller. Orange peel, knockdown, and acoustic finishes may be applied by roller, but are most often shot onto a primed surface from a spray gun with attached hopper. You can use a hand-powered spray texture pump. Or you can rent or purchase an air-powered spray texture gun.

For touching up small areas (less than 10 square feet), all of the above textures are available in aerosol spray cans.

TOUCHY TOUCH-UPS.

Regardless of the area involved, a seamless touch-up requires matching texture, color, and sheen.

Unless all three variables match those of the original finish, seams will be noticeable. Color is usually the most problematic—especially where a ceiling has been exposed to years of cigarette smoke.

Apply a stain-blocking primer, followed by a quality interior latex paint. The primer will block any smoke or water stains and provide maximum adhesion, while the top coat will provide uniform color and sheen.

TEXTURED REPAIR.

Acoustic (popcorn) texture presents a special repair problem. It is heavy and loses adhesion when wetted by latex paint. It can slide or even fall off a ceiling. The solution is to first prime the entire ceiling with white-pigmented shellac, then apply the repair with an aerosol spray can. After the repaired area dries, prime it a second time. The shellac primer provides a uniform base color and makes the textured material far more water resistant. As the final step, apply a latex flat or eggshell top coat.

The extreme texture of acoustic finish requires a roller with an extreme nap. Some fiber roller covers are known as acoustic rollers. Better yet, purchase a split-foam roller. Even with the special roller, however, the rule is, "Get in and get out as fast as you can." Apply the primer and paint in 2×2-foot areas: two strokes one way, followed by just two strokes at a right angle. Do not try to stretch the paint, and never go back.

TREATING STAINS AND MILDEW

IT WOULD ONLY SEEM FAIR that a fresh coat of paint, especially over a good primer, would cover stains, water marks, and mildew. In fact, when the paint is still wet, it may appear to cover. As it dries, however, these stains will seep through and you'll end up with a fresh coat of stained paint.

Before you prime or paint, remove stains and mildew. It takes elbow grease, but cleaning will save time in the long run because you won't have to repaint.

Although it adds time to a painting project, removing stains and mildew will save you frustration.

WATER LEACHES chemicals from wood and drywall. When the mixture seeps through a wall or ceiling, it stains.

MILDEW IS A SPORE in the air. Given food (paper or paint) and moisture, mildew flourishes.

STUFF YOU'LL NEED

TOOLS: Plastic bucket, rubber gloves, 4-foot stepladder, old clothes, safety goggles or glasses, large round-cornered sponge, rollers and brushes

MATERIALS: Water, household bleach, primer and paint, TSP solution

beware what you breathe

DON'T MIX BLEACH with other household cleaners. Household cleaners most often contain ammonia, which will react with the bleach to produce toxic fumes.

Inhaling such fumes can cause dizziness, nausea, cramps, or extreme illness. If you do breathe such fumes, get outside and breathe fresh air until your symptoms disappear.

 WORK SMARTER

what's the real problem?

ANYTIME MILDEW OR STAINS are present on your walls, they're signs of a larger problem. Find the source of the moisture that's causing the staining and get it fixed.

1 MIX THREE PARTS water to one part laundry bleach in a plastic bucket. If you are sensitive to bleach, protect your hands and eyes.

2 APPLY LIBERALLY with a sponge. Apply again after 20 minutes even if the mold has disappeared.

3 RINSE OFF the bleach and dead mildew with clean, fresh water. Allow it to dry thoroughly before cleaning with a TSP solution (see page 66), priming with a stain-blocking primer, and painting.

COMPLETE WALL PREP

Before painting, mark any marred wall areas with a soft-lead pencil so you don't overlook needed repairs.

NOW THAT YOU'VE REPAIRED THE DINGS AND DENTS, cleaned walls and ceilings of dirt, grease, and grime, and treated water stains and mildew, it is time to put all of that information to use to prepare a wall for painting.

First, move all furnishings away from the wall. Use a drop cloth to protect them from plaster dust, cleaning solutions, and inevitable paint spatters.

STUFF YOU'LL NEED

TOOLS: Bucket, rubber gloves, drop cloth, 4-foot stepladder, sponge, phillips screwdriver, 3-inch putty knife, sanding block, 2-inch nylon brush, 9-inch roller with ⅜-inch nap, roller tray

MATERIALS: 12-inch baseboard masking, blue painter's masking tape, bleach, water, lightweight crack filler, 220-grit sandpaper, oil-based, stain-blocking primer, TSP solution

1 **MOVE FURNITURE** away from walls and protect floor and baseboards with 12-inch baseboard masking and a paper/poly drop cloth.

2 **SET POPPED NAILS** or screws (page 60), repair cracks and holes (page 56–63), and fill dents with lightweight crack filler.

3 **TREAT ANY AREAS** of mildew with a 3-to-1 water/bleach solution (see page 65). Protect your hands with rubber gloves.

4 **RINSE THE ENTIRE** wall surface with clean, fresh water. Let the wall dry overnight. Clean with a TSP solution before you prime and paint.

CLOSE LOOK

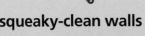

squeaky-clean walls

TRISODIUM PHOSPHATE (TSP), a nonsudsing soap, is the painter's cleaner of choice. Because it is 100 percent phosphate, TSP is the most powerful cleaner you can buy. But phosphate also causes algae blooms in water bodies, so its use has been restricted in some areas.

TSP will prevent paint from bonding, so rinse the surface several times with fresh water to remove all residue. Check the label for usage instructions.

TOOL TIP

wet-sanding

ONE OF THE MOST ANNOYING PARTS of sanding plaster and joint compound is the flour-like dust that is produced. To minimize the dust, use a drywall wet-sander: a sponge with coarse abrasive on one side and fine abrasive on the other side. Use the coarse side to level ridges and high spots; use the fine side to smooth.

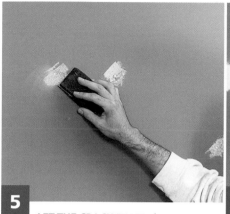

5 **LET THE CRACK FILLER** dry per manufacturer's instructions, then sand the wall using a sanding block with 220-grit sandpaper.

6 **SPOT PRIME** all of the repaired areas with a latex, stain-blocking primer. If stains are still bleeding through, use an oil-based primer.

7 **PRIME THE ENTIRE WALL** with the same stain-blocking primer for uniformity.

REMOVING GLOSS

IT IS ALMOST IMPOSSIBLE for paint to adhere to a glossy surface because a glossy surface lacks what painters call "tooth," or roughness, which gives the paint something to stick to. To detect gloss, use a bright light with a reflector to shield your eyes.

It doesn't take much to create tooth—a light sanding or use of a chemical deglosser will do the trick. When the surface ceases to be reflective, it's ready to paint.

OLD vs. NEW

liquid deglosser

IF THE PAINT IS SOUND and smooth enough that it doesn't require sanding, prepping with a liquid deglosser is a lot simpler. Be sure to follow the manufacturer's directions. Wear neoprene rubber gloves, goggles, and a respirator recommended by the deglosser manufacturer.

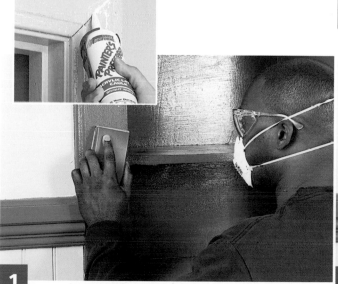

1 **FILL GAPS IN TRIM AND BASEBOARD WITH PAINTABLE CAULK, THEN SAND LIGHTLY** with 220-grit sandpaper. Use a sanding block for flat surfaces, a brass-wire brush for fluted surfaces.

2 **REMOVE THE SANDING** or brushing residue with a damp rag or tack cloth.

PRIMING IS ESSENTIAL

Priming the wall is the final step before you actually paint it.

WHY PRIME?

PRIMING HELPS ENSURE a professional-looking paint job. It isn't just a way to sell you one more paint product, and it isn't just watered-down paint. Primer is a specially formulated product designed to:

- Increase adhesion.
- Help the finish coat develop maximum sheen.
- Give the finish coat a uniform appearance.
- Increase the finish coat coverage.
- Block stains from water, dirt, smoke, etc.
- Block tannins from aromatic woods.
- Block resins from knots and pitch pockets.
- Add to corrosion resistance over metals.

PRIME NEW DRYWALL to conceal the difference between taped and untaped areas.

PRIME NEW WOOD, old bare wood, and pressure-treated lumber with a stain-killing primer to block resins and tannins in the wood and create a smooth and seamless finished surface. Let the primer dry thoroughly, according to the manufacturer's instructions, before applying finish color.

PRIME OVER WALLPAPER using a high-adhesion wallpaper primer. Make sure the old wallpaper is firmly attached to the wall and that rips, gouges, nicks, indentations, bulges, and tears are repaired. Make sure the walls are clean and smooth before you roll on the primer.

TYPES OF PRIMER

JUST AS PRIMER is different from finish paint, there are different primers for different problems and applications. **Apply all primers in adequate ventilation.**

1 POLYVINYL ACETATE (PVA) latex primer seals new drywall for painting. Both the paper face and joint compound are absorbent and would otherwise steal too much water from finish latex paint. It is not intended for trim or previously painted surfaces. Cleanup is with water.

2 ALL-PURPOSE PRIMER is a general term for any primer designed for maximum adhesion to impervious surfaces, such as metal, glass, tile, and thermoplastics, such as laminated plastic and melamine. It is harder to work with than a conventional latex primer, but the results are well worth the effort. Cleanup is with soap and water.

3 LATEX, STAIN-BLOCKING PRIMER is effective in stopping most staining materials from coming through the paint. For difficult stains, such as washable markers, use oil-based or alcohol-based primer instead.

4 OIL-BASED, STAIN-BLOCKING PRIMER effectively blocks crayon, permanent-marker inks, grease, and water stains. Even though it is a bit harder to work with, the results are worth the effort—it's one of the rare ways to prevent an unremovable stain from bleeding through paint. Cleanup is with paint thinner.

5 ALCOHOL-BASED, WHITE-PIGMENTED SHELLAC is impervious, exhibits excellent adhesion, and effectively blocks smoke stains and all of the tannins and resins in wood. It is brittle and damaged by UV rays, however, so it is recommended only for interior use. The exception is spot-priming knots on pine trim and clapboards. Clean up with denatured alcohol. Also inhibits pet odors.

6 ENAMEL UNDERCOAT contains a higher percentage of solids and is used when maximum effect is desired in satin, semigloss, or gloss. Being hard, it can be sanded to produce the smoothest possible base for the finish coat. Cleanup is with soap and water.

HOMER'S HINDSIGHT

prime mistake

ABOUT FOUR UNNECESSARY COATS of an expensive designer color later, I learned the hard way that flat latex paint isn't a primer. It pays to follow the instructions and believe what they told you in the paint store about proper preparation.

CLOSER LOOK

why use both paint and primer?

PAINT AND PRIMER perform two distinct and important functions, and to get a good job you can't use one without the other. Primer provides bonding and blocking. Paint provides durability and color.

WORK SMARTER

prime info on dark colors

IT SEEMS LOGICAL THAT darker colors hide better. It's not true. When painting a dark, rich color, you've got to use a tinted primer and at least two coats of paint to get a good look.

PRIMING WALLS AND TRIM

After you've done the repairs and cleaned the walls, you're ready to prime.

STUFF YOU'LL NEED

TOOLS: Paint can opener or screwdriver, stirring stick, 2-inch brush, 9-inch roller with appropriate nap, roller extension handle, 4-foot stepladder, drywall sanding block

MATERIALS: Primer (different types for wall and trim), 12-inch baseboard masking, blue painter's masking tape, 220-grit sandpaper

PRIMED FOR SUCCESS

PRIMING INVOLVES the same steps as painting the finish coat on the wall.

To prepare all surfaces for priming, first repair and clean them. Cover all surfaces you do not plan to paint; primer can be as difficult to remove as paint. And it spatters just as well!

Timing is critical when you're priming and painting. It is best to apply the finish paint within a day or two of priming. This will minimize the sanding, and ensure that the primer has enough tooth for the paint to adhere.

1 **MOST PRIMERS** can be tinted, and tinting will ensure good coverage with the finish coat. But too much tint will dilute the primer and reduce its efficiency. Usually a primer can be tinted by no more than half; follow the recommendations of the manufacturer.

2 **PROTECT THE BASEBOARDS** with 12-inch baseboard masking.

GOOD IDEA

the tape test

If the wall has been previously painted with latex, if there has been no patching, and if the paint is clean and adhering well, you may be able to consider the old paint to be the primer for the new.

Here is a test: Press a piece of transparent tape onto the old paint, then remove it. If the old paint comes off with the tape, you need to prime.

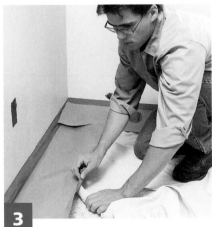

3 **TUCK A PAPER/POLY** drop cloth under the baseboard masking for complete floor coverage.

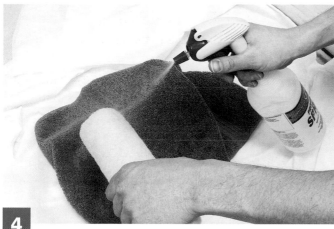

4 **DAMPEN YOUR ROLLER** or brush to get off to a fast start. Use water for latex, paint thinner for alkyd.

5 **PICK YOUR STARTING POINT** and cut in the corner with a 2-inch sash brush or a corner pad. Cut in the first 3 to 4 feet of the ceiling too.

6 **APPLY THE PRIMER** using a 9-inch roller with the appropriate nap. Start with a single vertical strip at the cut-in corner.

7 **ROLL THE REMAINING WALL** in 3×3-foot sections, working from top to bottom. Lay the primer down in a W, then fill in the gaps without lifting the roller.

8 **AFTER THE PRIMER DRIES,** some manufacturers recommend lightly sanding the primed wall with 220-grit sandpaper and a drywall sanding block. If recommended, sand as needed.

PRIMING TRIM

1. AFTER THE WALL is thoroughly dry, mask the wall at the edges of the trim with blue painter's masking tape.

2. LIGHTLY SAND THE TRIM (see page 67), then apply the appropriate primer with a bristle brush sized for painting trim.

4 ROOM PAINTING BASICS

IN THIS SECTION: the transformation

IT'S TIME TO PAINT! Here are step-by-step instructions for success when you paint ceilings, walls, floors, windows, doors, and trim. There are special tips to ensure success at painting a variety of surfaces. You'll also find a troubleshooting guide to help you avoid common mistakes—or recognize and repair them.

WELL-PAINTED TRIM adds a simple finishing touch to the dramatic effect of the color wash on the walls. A good paint job is the result of taking the time to execute each step in the painting process carefully.

PAINTING CEILINGS

Ceilings are as easy to paint as the walls. Just do the necessary prep work and use the right tools.

STUFF YOU'LL NEED

TOOLS: Screwdriver, utility knife, paint pad, 9-inch roller cover with the appropriate nap, roller cage with extension handle, paint tray, 4-foot stepladder, safety goggles, painter's cap

MATERIALS: Plastic bag(s), 2-inch painter's masking tape, paper/poly drop cloth, latex ceiling paint, clean cotton rag

PAINTING A CEILING? Invest in an extension pole, safety goggles, and a painter's cap. And use ceiling—not wall—paint. It comes in a variety of colors, all specially formulated to:

■ Diffuse light from lamps, windows, and other sources of illumination.

■ Have a flat sheen so the ceiling will have an even appearance.

■ Offer better spatter resistance for overhead rolling.

Prep the ceiling before you paint it. Dust and grime accumulate, making it virtually impossible for paint to adhere. Mildew and water stains will bleed through even the best of paint. Cracks, mars, and dents are more visible in the artificial light that generally reflects off ceilings.

Keys to superior ceiling results are careful, thorough preparation, priming, and the use of quality paint.

Add color. The ceiling can be an important part of your color palette. For instance, if you want to bring the ceiling "down" for a cozier room, paint it a darker color. For a light, airy feeling, paint the ceiling the lightest hue of blue.

1 **REMOVE FURNITURE FROM THE ROOM.** Shut off overhead fixtures at the breaker or fuse box.

2 **REMOVE OR BAG THE CEILING FIXTURES.** Removal of the ceiling fixtures will make for a neater job, but you can also drop the cover plates and wrap the fixtures in plastic bags.

WORK SMARTER

extension poles

EXTENSION POLES MAKE PAINTING ceilings easier and more efficient. Poles that extend from 4 to 6 feet will allow you to roll the majority of the ceiling without having to use a ladder. The pole should be long enough that you can hold the bottom at hip level and the top at head level. Extension poles make rolling walls easier as well.

BUYER'S GUIDE

a good investment

MUCH OF THE MESS when painting a ceiling is from the drips that come when you're reaching from bucket to ceiling. A power roller eliminates the extra motion as well as most drips—and speeds up things!

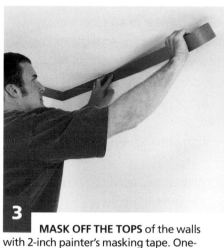

3 **MASK OFF THE TOPS** of the walls with 2-inch painter's masking tape. One-inch tape would allow the roller to strike the wall.

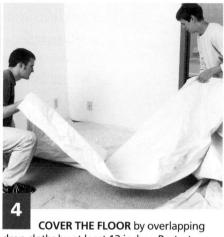

4 **COVER THE FLOOR** by overlapping drop cloths by at least 12 inches. Protect windows, doors, and trim, if necessary.

5 **PRIME THE ROLLER COVER** by spraying it with a misting bottle until it is just damp. Remove excess water before you begin painting.

6 **TO START, CUT IN ONE CORNER** of the ceiling with a paint pad. Cut in only as much as you can roll out before the paint dries.

7 **BEGIN ROLLING OVER** the still-wet cut-in strip. Keeping a wet edge prevents overlap marks in the finished ceiling. Load the roller regularly and roll slowly. Backroll to blend the paint.

8 **WORK IN SECTIONS** to keep wet edges. Cut in with a pad or brush, apply paint with a roller, then roll out applied paint to blend the two areas.

GOOD IDEA

better results

Roll in the direction of the shorter room dimension to minimize the drying time between passes. This gives you time to feather the wet paint, avoiding overlap marks.

PAINTING CEILINGS (continued)

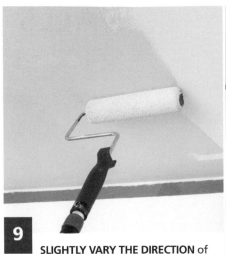

9   **SLIGHTLY VARY THE DIRECTION** of your rolling. Perfectly straight rolling is more likely to show overlap marks.

10   **CONTINUE APPLYING PAINT,** rolling out and blending until the first cut-in section is finished.

11   **BEGIN THE NEXT SECTION** by cutting in the wall/ceiling joint.

12   **APPLY PAINT,** roll out, and blend with the cut-in edge and the previous section.

13   **KEEP AN EYE OPEN** for drips and spatters. Wipe up immediately with a damp rag.

PAINTING POPCORN CEILINGS

POPCORN CEILINGS have a water-soluble base so water-based paints can cause the popcorn texture to come down as you roll on the paint. Before painting, the ceiling should be sealed with a white-pigmented shellac.

Always paint with flat paint. Work the paint on in 2-foot squares with light pressure, crosshatch in one direction only, and don't reroll. Once a section is finished move on. For more information on painting and repairing textured ceilings, see page 64.

BUYER'S GUIDE

use the right roller for popcorn ceilings

POPCORN CEILINGS REQUIRE special rollers that will allow the paint to fill in properly. Depending on the thickness of the popcorn, use a thick-napped or split-foam roller. See the experts at your home or paint center for more information.

PAINTING WALLS

CHANGING THE COLOR SCHEME IN A ROOM is the quickest and least expensive decorating touch on the market.

A quality wall paint is formulated to:
- Provide maximum hiding.
- Have good scrub and burnish resistance.
- Resist stains from spills, ink markers, and crayons.

If you are radically changing the colors, or are applying a much darker color, a second coat is essential and a third may be necessary to completely cover a wall.

Start painting from a corner of the room that isn't hit by direct sunlight. Sunlit walls may be too hot for the paint to make its initial bond and could affect the final cure. If the wall is warm to the touch, wait until it cools down before you apply the paint.

The basics of painting are easy to learn, and putting them into practice will make every painting job easier and faster!

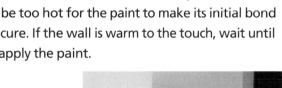

STUFF YOU'LL NEED

TOOLS: Screwdriver, utility knife, 2-inch trim nylon or polyester brush, 9-inch roller cover with ⅜-inch nap, roller cage with extension handle, paint tray, 4-foot stepladder

MATERIALS: Paint test panels or sheet of drywall, painter's masking tape, 12-inch baseboard masking, paper/poly drop cloth, latex wall paint, clean cotton rag

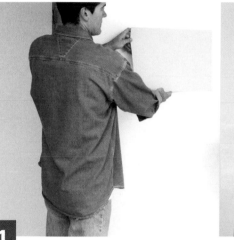
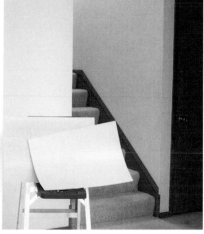

1   **BEFORE FINALIZING YOUR WALL COLOR SELECTION,** paint several test panels. Purchase blank test panels from a paint center or make them from cut-up drywall. Compare candidate colors under all the lighting conditions you will find in the room over the course of a full day and evening.

2   **REMOVE ALL** of the electrical cover plates on the wall by removing the screws.

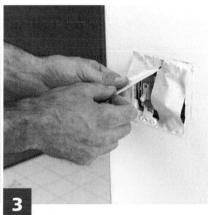

3   **PULL OFF DIMMER KNOBS.** Cover the switches and receptacles with painter's masking tape.

WORK SMARTER

estimating square footage

THE PROS RECOMMEND coverage of no more than 300 to 400 square feet per gallon for good results. See the front of this book for a helpful guide to calculating how much paint you'll need for your room.

4 **REMOVE ALL** of the furniture or group it in the center of the room. Protect it from spatters with plastic or a drop cloth.

5 **MASK ANY SURFACES** not to be painted, such as door and window casings, with blue painter's masking tape.

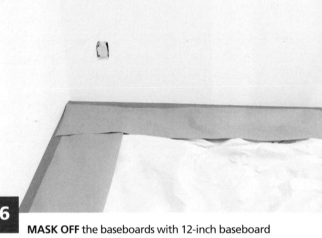

6 **MASK OFF** the baseboards with 12-inch baseboard masking, overlapping the floor drop cloth.

7 **BOX THE PAINT** (mix the contents of all the containers for consistency) in a 5-gallon bucket and stir.

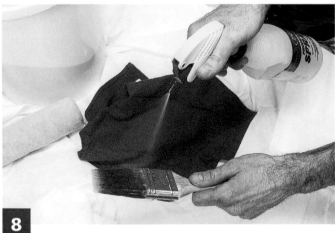

8 **PRIME THE ROLLER COVER** and cutting-in brush by wetting with a misting bottle. Remove excess water before applying paint.

9 **START BY CUTTING IN** a corner with the brush. Cut in only as far as your arm will reach to make sure you keep a wet edge when you roll on the paint.

10 **BEGIN ROLLING** by applying a vertical strip that overlaps the cut-in strip.

11 **ROLL PAINT** in a 3×3-foot W pattern, then spread the paint to fill in the pattern. Continue in 3×3-foot sections and back-roll (see Step 12) until you're finished.

12 **BACK-ROLL AS YOU GO.** Fill the roller with a light load and roll the wet paint from floor to ceiling to blend and finish each section. Apply subsequent coats as needed.

13 **GIVE THE WALL PAINT** a minimum of 24 hours to cure, then mask with blue painter's masking tape. If the wall isn't fully cured, mask with white quick-release tape so you won't remove paint when you remove the tape.

GOOD IDEA

stop smart

Always finish a painting session at a natural divide (an inside or outside corner or a doorway). The differences in lighting prevent your eye from detecting subtle changes in color or sheen that may occur when you continue painting later.

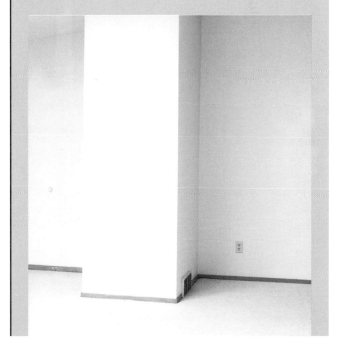

14 **PAINT THE TRIM** as shown on pages 92–95. Remove the tape immediately to avoid lifting the paint off the wall.

PAINTING WOOD FLOORS

Specially formulated paints can help you include your floor in your overall color scheme.

STUFF YOU'LL NEED

TOOLS: Hammer, nail set, drill, power screwdriver, putty knife, pad sander, dust-resistant mask, vacuum cleaner, sponge mop, 1-inch throwaway brush, 1½-inch polyester sash brush, 5-gallon bucket, 1-quart measure, 9-inch roller cover with ⅜-inch nap, roller cage with extension handle, paint tray

MATERIALS: 1¼-inch drywall screws, wood glue, wood shims, latex wood filler, 80-grit sandpaper, blue painter's masking tape, floor paint

IN COLONIAL DAYS, paint was the finish of choice to decorate floors. Today, with wear-resistant formulations, paint is an even more appropriate selection for specific floor challenges. Once again, good preparation and the right product are the keys.

Paint often provides the best solution when you don't want wall-to-wall carpet and the existing floor is not that attractive. Plywood floors and wood floors that have been patched with different sizes and species of wood are among the best candidates.

Another option is to consider the floor a blank canvas and create a decorative pattern. (See page 98 for information on painting masonry floors.)

PAINTED WOOD FLOORS are traditional in Early American and country homes and can be as attractive as those with clear finish.

BUYER'S GUIDE

floors aren't walls

PAINTS DESIGNED to work on vertical surfaces won't do the job horizontally. Choose paints designated for use on floors and porches. They are generally available in semigloss and gloss sheens and are formulated specifically for use on horizontal surfaces. Carefully follow the manufacturer's recommendations for application.

GOOD IDEA

cover it up

There are several reasons to paint a wood floor, such as covering unsightly repair work or concealing unattractive old varnish. Plus, painting a floor is far less expensive than carpeting it.

1 **REMOVE ALL OF THE FURNITURE** from the room. It makes the job easier.

2 **DRIVE PROTRUDING** nailheads just below the surface using a hammer and a nail set. If the floor squeaks and you can't get access to the subfloor from below, drive longer nails into the joists from the top.

3 **IF THE FLOOR SQUEAKS** and you can get to the subfloor, drill several pilot holes through from below, and fasten the spot with drywall screws from beneath. Make sure the screws aren't too long.

4 **IF THE SQUEAK PERSISTS,** mark the location while someone walks across the floor, and drive glued wedges between the subfloor and the joist.

5 **FILL ANY CRACKS WIDER** than ⅛ inch with latex wood filler. Read the label to make sure the product will expand and contract with the wood and is formulated to accept paint.

6 **IF THE FLOOR** is in rough shape, sand it with a floor sander. Otherwise sand it lightly with a pad sander using 80- or 100-grit sandpaper. Wear a dust-resistant mask while sanding.

7 **VACUUM** the sanding dust. This will also help you find protruding nailheads. The floor must be dust-free when you paint.

PAINTING WOOD FLOORS (continued)

8 **DAMP-MOP** the floor with clean water to remove dust, which will interfere with paint adhesion.

9 **MASK THE BASEBOARDS,** including any heating units, all around the floor with blue painter's masking tape.

10 **IF THE FLOOR IS PINE** and contains knots, spot prime the knots with white-pigmented shellac.

11 **IF THE FLOOR IS BARE WOOD** or a composition wood product, apply sanding sealer before priming.

12 **MAKE THE PRIMER** by diluting the finish floor paint by 25 percent (1 quart per gallon) with water if using an acrylic latex floor paint, or with paint thinner if using an alkyd paint.

13 **CUT IN THE PRIMER AROUND** the baseboards with a 1½- or 2-inch angled sash brush.

paint under the right conditions

■ Paint at the temperature and humidity recommended by the manufacturer.

■ Provide airflow to promote even drying.

■ Allow the paint to dry thoroughly between coats and cure fully before use.

14   **STARTING IN A CORNER,** apply the rest of the primer using a 9-inch roller cover with a ⅜-inch nap.

15   **FOR THE SMOOTHEST** result, always roll in the direction of the flooring.

16   **DON'T PAINT YOURSELF** into a corner; plan ahead so you end up in the doorway out of the room.

17   **AFTER THE PRIMER** dries (read the manufacturer's instructions), cut in the full-strength finish coat.

18   **APPLY THE FINISH COAT OF PAINT** in the same way and pattern as the primer. You can use the same roller cover.

ROOM PAINTING BASICS

PAINTING WINDOWS

A room isn't finished until the windows look as good as the walls. Here's how to do it.

STUFF YOU'LL NEED

TOOLS: Utility knife, two sawhorses or a bench, putty knife, orbital sander, caulk gun, 1-inch polyester sash brush

MATERIALS: Rubber gloves, TSP solution, 80- and 220-grit sandpaper, latex wood putty, paintable acrylic latex caulk, 1-inch blue painter's masking tape, sponge, plastic scrub pad, 100 percent acrylic latex primer, latex enamel paint

WINDOWS ARE ESSENTIAL to most room designs, and basic to the appearance of a window is the quality of its finish. A window with delicate molding separating panes and a smooth semigloss finish denotes elegance. The same window, chipped and peeling with paint spilling onto the glass, is shabby.

Wooden windows take a beating. They are exposed year-round to sun, wind, and rain, and are constantly opened and closed. Regular maintenance provides windows with a longer life and a better appearance.

Painting windows takes patience. Cutting in the small strips and corners can be time-consuming. Use a top-quality brush to make your job easier and produce a more professional result.

Don't scrimp on preparation. Sand even a sound finish to ensure adhesion of the new paint. And if the old finish is chipped or peeling, scrape and sand it until no ridges are apparent.

IF THE SASH IS PAINTED SHUT

1 **CUT THROUGH** the paint with a utility knife. After several passes, try wedging the sash up from outside with a flat bar.

2 **IF THE UTILITY KNIFE** doesn't work, use a grout saw or metal-cutting hacksaw blade secured in locking pliers.

HOMER'S HINDSIGHT

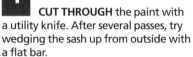

don't paint it shut

A MARK OF THE UNINITIATED is painting the crack between the window sash and frame. It may help if you are trying to eliminate all air infiltration. But it's a terrible mistake if you plan to ever open the window again.

To avoid painting a window closed, apply paint to the sash and the frame in two separate strokes. Minimize the amount of paint you apply at the joint. Move the sash up and down a few times as the paint dries.

3 **REMOVE THE SASH** by popping it out or removing the screws that hold the sash molding in place.

4 **PLACE THE SASH** flat across a pair of sawhorses or on a workbench.

5 **SCRUB THE SASH** with TSP solution using a plastic scrub pad. Rinse thoroughly. Use soap and water on aluminum windows—TSP solution will etch the metal and ruin the window.

6 **SCRAPE TO REMOVE** all loose paint, then sand with 80-and then 220-grit sandpaper to smooth the ridges. Wear a dust-resistant mask.

7 **FILL HOLES OR DENTS** with wood putty and a putty knife. Sand until smooth with 220-grit sandpaper.

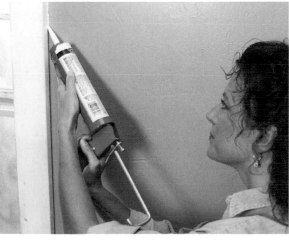

8 **FILL ANY CRACKS** between the window casing and the wall with caulk that is formulated to accept paint. Be sure to remove old paint from the cracks and dust clean.

PAINTING WINDOWS (continued)

9   **AFTER THE CAULK CURES** (24 hours minimum), mask the walls with 1-inch blue painter's tape.

10   **MASK THE GLASS PANES** with blue painter's tape, leaving a $\frac{1}{32}$-inch gap between the trim and the glass so that the paint will seal the glass, then replace the sash in its frame.

11   **APPLY PRIMER** to the muntins with an angled sash brush. Tinting the primer the same color as the finish may save a coat.

12   **RAISE THE BOTTOM** and lower the top sashes, and prime the sash horizontals.

13   **PRIME THE SASH VERTICALS,** minimizing the amount of primer that spills over onto the casings.

14   **PRIME THE CASINGS,** again minimizing overlap with sashes. Move the sashes to break the paint line.

15 COMPLETE THE WINDOW by priming the sill and apron, moving the sash up and down occasionally until the primer is dry to make sure the window doesn't stick.

16 AFTER THE TIME specified by the primer manufacturer, apply the finish coat in the same order you applied the primer. Remove the painter's tape when you have finished painting. Apply two finish coats on the window sill and trim as well.

PAINTING VINYL WINDOWS

YES, YOU CAN CHANGE the color of a vinyl window. The keys are thorough cleaning, proper surface preparation, and quality materials.

Wearing rubber gloves, wash the vinyl with a TSP solution. Take special care with small corners and crevices where dust settles.

For paint to adhere, vinyl needs "tooth." Scrub it with a plastic abrasive scrub pad. When you finish, gently dust the surface. You want to remove residual particles, not repolish the vinyl surface, so go easy.

Be sure the primer has time to cure completely before you apply the finish coat.

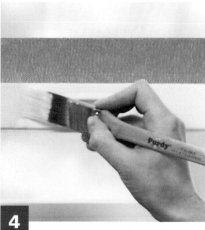

1 WASH THE VINYL THOROUGHLY with a TSP solution to remove any grease or oily film.

2 SCRUB ALL SURFACES with a plastic abrasive scrub pad. Use enough pressure to give the smooth vinyl "tooth."

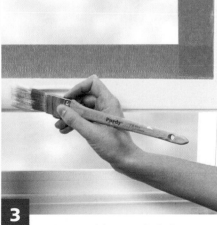

3 PRIME, as with a wood window, using high-quality latex primer.

4 APPLY A FINISH COAT of high-quality latex enamel paint.

PAINTING DOORS

Here's how to prepare and paint a door so the finish coat will look beautiful and adhere tenaciously.

STUFF YOU'LL NEED

TOOLS: Screwdriver, utility knife, two sawhorses, large 2-handed scraper, pad sander or sanding block, power screwdriver, caulk gun, 1½-inch polyester sash brush, 2-inch polyester trim brush

MATERIALS: TSP solution, masking tape, 80-, 220-, and 320-grit sandpaper, four 3-inch drywall screws, white-pigmented shellac (if door has knots), 100 percent acrylic latex primer, latex enamel paint

GOOD IDEA

roller option

Some professional painters feel that the best tool for getting a smooth coat on a door is a "cigar" or "hot dog" roller. This dense foam roller is 6 inches long and results in a smooth finish coat without brush marks. You will still need to brush in the bevels in the door panels.

THE DOOR IS A FOCAL POINT of any wall and has a dynamic impact on the overall decor in a room.

Most doors see a lot of use—even a bit of abuse. (Think of the fingerprints and kick marks!) Proper, thorough preparation is the first—and most important—step of the process. Filling dings and dents along with sanding and priming so the finish will adhere properly may take up to 80 percent of the time you will spend on the project.

If the door will be finished in different colors on opposite sides, make sure you will see the correct edge color when the door is open, as well as when it is closed (see "Closer Look" on page 90).

Use a gloss or semigloss finish to help repel fingerprints. Use a good-quality paint that will stand up to frequent scrubbing.

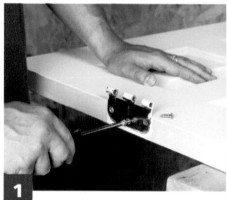

1 **REMOVE THE DOOR,** then remove the hinge leaves from the door edge. Wash the door with a TSP solution and rinse.

2 **APPLY MASKING TAPE** and trim with a utility knife to fill the hinge mortises. If there is paint in a mortise, the door may stick.

3 **REMOVE BLISTERED** or chipped paint with a sharp paint scraper. Use both hands and apply even, firm pressure. Be careful not to gouge the wood.

4 **SAND THE CHIP RIDGES** smooth with 80-grit sandpaper. Follow up with 220-grit sandpaper so the sanding marks won't show under the finish.

5

DRIVE ONE 3-INCH drywall screw halfway into each of the door's top and bottom edges. Make sure the screws are in far enough to hold the weight of the door on the sawhorses.

6

SUSPEND THE DOOR on sawhorses from the four screws so the entire side can be painted at the same time.

CLOSER LOOK

orderly painting

TO MINIMIZE BRUSH MARKS, paint your door in the order shown below. Painting sections from top to bottom will give you the time you need to feather each application of paint before it dries. Paint all the edges first and then areas 2 through 5 in each section of the door before you move on.

It is possible to paint a door without removing it from the jamb, but the order below is critical to avoid drips that inevitably occur when you're painting vertically.

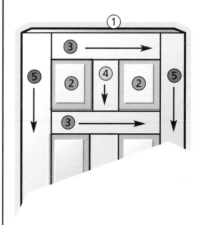

PAINTING ORDER

1. All edges
2. Panel bevels and panel flats
3. Rails
4. Stile middles
5. Stiles

7

PRIME THE DOOR, applying the primer in the order shown above in "Closer Look."

8

AFTER THE TIME SPECIFIED by the primer manufacturer, sand lightly with 220-grit sandpaper.

9 **FIRST PAINT THE DOOR EDGES.** Don't worry about the screws on the top and bottom corners; they won't be seen.

10 **NEXT PAINT THE BEVELED** areas of the raised panels. Use a 1- or 1½-inch sash brush, depending on the bevel width.

11 **PAINT THE PANEL FLATS** using a 2-inch sash brush. Blend lightly with the beveled areas.

12 **CHECK FOR AND SMOOTH DRIPS** on the panels and bevels. Then paint straight across the top rail.

13 **PAINT THE STILES** from the top down to the next rail, blending paint with the top rail.

CLOSE LOOK

at a glance

A DOOR DEFINES TWO DECORS: The area it provides entry to, and the area it leaves. So it is not unusual for a door to be painted two colors. Each side is finished to enhance the decor of the room it faces when the door is closed. The question is, what color should the edges be painted?

Paint the edges of the door to match the side that is visible when the door is open or closed, as shown in the illustration at right. The result will be an increased sense of visual continuity between rooms of different colors and/or decors.

■ COLOR A
□ COLOR B

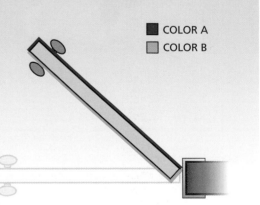

14 ALTERNATE PAINTING RAILS AND STILES until you reach and finish the bottom rail. Don't attempt to touch up. If you have a problem, repaint the entire rail or stile after it's dry.

15 PAINT THE LONG STILES, feathering the paint between each stroke. Catch drips and runs as you paint.

UNFINISHED FIR AND PINE DOORS

MOST WOODEN DOORS need to be sanded before they can be finished. If the door has a rough finish, start by sanding with 80-grit sandpaper. Then finish sanding with 220-grit sandpaper. Use a hand sander for best results. Be sure to remove all dust before you start priming or painting.

1 SAND AN UNFINISHED DOOR with 220-grit sandpaper and then with 320-grit if it needs further finishing. Remove all dust with a lint-free cloth.

2 IF THE DOOR is unfinished pine, spot prime all of the knots with white-pigmented shellac.

RUST SPOTS ON STEEL DOORS

1. METAL DOORS often rust at the bottom because of salt on sidewalks. Remove loose rust with 80-grit emery cloth. Feather the edges so there isn't a ridge between old paint and unpainted metal.

2. PAINT OVER remaining rust and bare metal with a liquid rust converter. Use paint that is specifically formulated for metal doors. Blend new paint with old to avoid a paint ridge.

PAINTING TRIM

Trim outlines a room and enhances the special features in it. Follow these steps for a fitting finish.

STUFF YOU'LL NEED

TOOLS: Utility knife, plastic scrub pad, large sponge, 2-handed paint scraper, pad sander or sanding block, putty knife, caulk gun, 1½-inch polyester sash brush, 2-inch polyester trim brush, rubber gloves

MATERIALS: TSP solution, blue painter's masking tape, 80- and 220-grit sandpaper, latex wood putty, acrylic-latex caulk, lightweight crack filler, denatured alcohol, cotton rag, white-pigmented shellac, stain sealer, 100 percent acrylic latex primer, latex enamel paint, chemical deglosser (optional)

WHETHER YOU ARE PAINTING DOORS, windows, baseboards, or moldings, there are four key steps to success:

- Cleaning and priming to achieve maximum adhesion.
- Smoothing the surface so that cracks, holes, dents, and chips don't show through the finish coat.
- Masking adjacent surfaces so you can paint quickly and confidently.
- Keeping a wet edge to eliminate lap marks.

When you are painting trim, the critical tools are the paintbrushes. You will need:

- An angled sash brush for laying down sharp edges.
- A square-edged trim brush for laying down flat areas of paint.
- An oval brush for getting into tight areas.

1 **OILY FILMS FROM COOKING** prevent adhesion, so wash woodwork with a TSP solution and a plastic scrub pad.

2 **RINSE AREAS WASHED** with TSP several times because any residue will also reduce adhesion.

GOOD
IDEA

unstick it

If a door sticks, planing it to a smaller size will generally unstick it. Before you take this time-consuming step, realize that it is probably not the door that has grown. A door usually sticks because the door has loosened from the framing.

The simple cure is to drive 16d common nails (or 3-inch drywall screws) just above and below each of the hinges to pull the frame back to its original position.

If you have a sticky door, try this first. It works!

3 USE BOTH HANDS to scrape blistered or chipped paint. Take care not to gouge the wood.

4 ELIMINATE THE EDGES of chipped areas with 80-grit, then 220-grit sandpaper. Remove dust with a lint-free cloth.

5 FILL ANY GOUGES OR DENTS with wood putty. Shape to conform to the shape of the molding.

6 FILL NAIL HOLES with window painter's putty, glazing compound, or another lightweight filler. Remove excess material and let the material dry per the manufacturer's instructions.

7 FILL GAPS AND CRACKS between trim pieces with paintable caulk. Cut the tip of the caulking tube to flow a ⅛-inch bead of caulk into the gap in the trim.

8 **SMOOTH THE CAULK** by wetting your index finger and running it over the surface.

9 **FINISH SANDING THE ENTIRE** area with 220-grit sandpaper or wipe with a chemical deglosser.

10 **WIPE THE SANDED** or deglossed woodwork with a rag soaked in denatured alcohol. Wear protective gloves.

11 **MASK ALL ADJACENT** surfaces with blue painter's masking tape. Seal the edges firmly.

12 **SPOT PRIME** any knots or resin pockets with white-pigmented shellac primer. Allow to dry.

CLOSER LOOK

trim colors

WHEN YOU'RE PAINTING DOOR TRIM, there seems to be a choice: Paint it the color of the door open or closed.

Trim should be painted to coordinate with the room itself, not the adjacent areas. Paint the trim the same color as the closed door on that side.

Close the door. Paint the trim to match (or coordinate with) the closed door. The result will be a sense of visual continuity that enhances your decor.

■ COLOR A
□ COLOR B

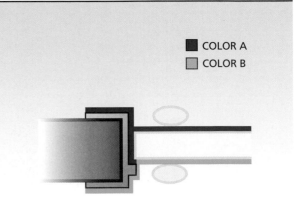

13 **PRIME THE ENTIRE SURFACE** with a stain sealer recommended by your paint center.

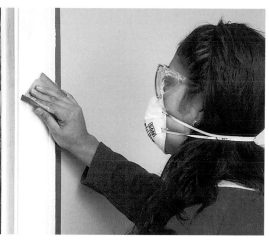

14 **AFTER 24 HOURS,** sand the primed surface with 220-grit sandpaper. Hold the paper with your fingers if the molding is irregular; you'll have less trouble getting into the corners.

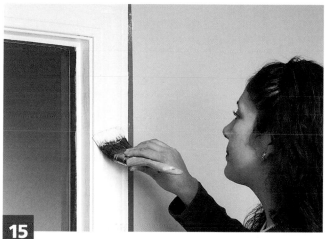

15 **WIPE THE SANDED SURFACE** with a damp sponge or rag, then apply the finish with a 2-inch trim brush.

16 **REMOVE THE MASKING TAPE** while the paint is still wet so it won't pull paint from the trim.

STAIN-BLOCKING PRIMERS

1. STAIN-BLOCKING PRIMERS AND SEALERS may still show the stain because they absorb, rather than cover, the stain. Use a stain-blocker before you prime; allow it to dry thoroughly. This will help ensure that stubborn stains don't bleed through, ruining an otherwise perfect finish.

2. HAVE THE PRIMER TINTED especially when you make a dramatic color change. Remember that there are limitations on the amount of tint a primer can hold and still be effective. Follow the manufacturer's recommendations.

QUICK TIP For best results, make sure you keep your working area within the proper temperature range recommended for the paint.

PAINTING PLASTIC LAMINATE

Old cabinets can look new again with a fresh coat of paint. Add some new hardware and it's almost like treating yourself to a brand-new kitchen.

STUFF YOU'LL NEED

TOOLS: Utility knife, screwdriver, large sponge, pad sander or sanding block, small paint pad or 2-inch polyester trim brush, rubber gloves

MATERIALS: TSP solution, 220-grit sandpaper, clean cotton cloth, denatured alcohol, bonding primer, latex enamel paint

WORK SMARTER

number the doors

NUMBER THE CABINET DOORS and openings as you remove them so you'll be able to rehang them in the right opening.

QUICK TIP Have a container of some kind handy to hold all the hardware and screws as you remove them from the cabinets. It's nice to be able to reinstall all the pieces you took off when you're finished painting.

THE PLASTIC LAMINATE CABINETS in your kitchen or bath can take on a new look. It's a myth that paint won't stick to such plastics. Paint will adhere to virtually any surface, as long as it is clean and has "tooth" (surface roughness). Your challenge is to thoroughly clean the cabinets, give the surface tooth, prime the cabinets, and paint them properly.

If you take the time to perform each critical step of the preparation, you will be rewarded with a set of cabinets that look like new, especially if you replace the old knobs. Home centers carry a large selection of replacement knobs, and if you're looking for something really special, search hardware sites online.

BEFORE

AFTER

PAINTED CABINETS are traditional in Early American and country homes. They are attractive and enhance your color selection!

1 **REMOVE THE CABINET DOORS.** Achieving a smooth finish is always simpler when the painted surface is horizontal.

2 **REMOVE ANY HARDWARE** (knobs, pulls, hinges, and catches) that you would have to sand or paint around.

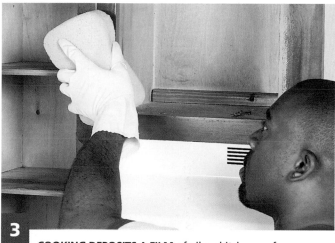

3 **COOKING DEPOSITS A FILM** of oil on kitchen surfaces, so scrub with a TSP solution. Rinse thoroughly with fresh water.

4 **TO GIVE THE HARD PLASTIC** surface "tooth," sand with 220-grit sandpaper until the finish is completely dulled.

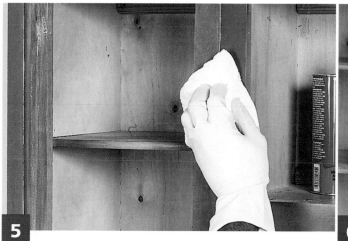

5 **WIPE OFF THE POWDER RESIDUE** with a clean cotton cloth dampened in denatured alcohol. Wear protective gloves.

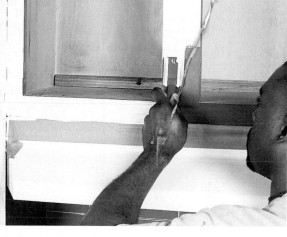

6 **APPLY A WHITE-PIGMENTED SHELLAC-BASED OR ENAMEL UNDERCOAT PRIMER** with the roller, paint pad, or brush recommended by the manufacturer.

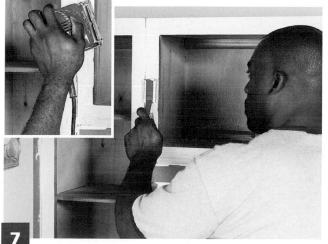

7 **LIGHTLY SAND THE PRIMED SURFACE** with 220-grit sandpaper, remove the dust with a damp rag, and apply a coat of gloss or semigloss paint within 24 hours. A second finish coat may be necessary.

HOMER'S HINDSIGHT

I've got the cabinet knob blues

I SPENT OVER A WEEK PREPPING AND PAINTING the kitchen cabinets. I even got new hardware and knobs for a serious kitchen redo. But when I attached the first knob on the most visible cabinet door in the kitchen, I held the screw from the back and turned the knob until it was tight. In the process I tore a jagged chunk of paint off the cabinet door. So hold the knob lightly against the surface and use a screwdriver to tighten the screw in place.

PAINTING CONCRETE MASONRY

Paint is attractive and hardworking on a concrete floor when you follow these steps.

STUFF YOU'LL NEED

TOOLS: Garden hose, garden sprayer or spray bottle, scissors or utility knife, plastic bucket, rubber boots, stiff floor scrub brush, 9-inch roller cover with ⅜-inch nap, roller cage with extension handle

MATERIALS: Duct tape, 4×4-foot square of poly sheeting, TSP solution, sulfamic acid, concrete stain or paint

WORK SMARTER

read the warranty

FLOOR PAINT MANUFACTURERS have very specific guidelines for application of their products. If you don't follow them exactly, you can end up with a bad paint job and void the warranty at the same time.

CONCRETE POSES THREE CHALLENGES not encountered when painting other surfaces:

■ Concrete is porous and usually in contact with soil, so water vapor pressure may pose a problem.

■ Oil and gasoline are often spilled and left on driveways and garage floors. They are petrochemicals, which can soften solvent-based paints.

■ Hot rubber tires can bond to and lift driveway and garage floor paints that are not formulated to resist "hot-tire pickup."

If you are painting concrete other than a driveway or garage floor, make sure you use a paint that is specifically formulated for concrete. Follow the manufacturer's directions exactly.

If the concrete surface will be subject to hot tires, specify a paint that is formulated to resist hot-tire pickup, chemicals, and oils.

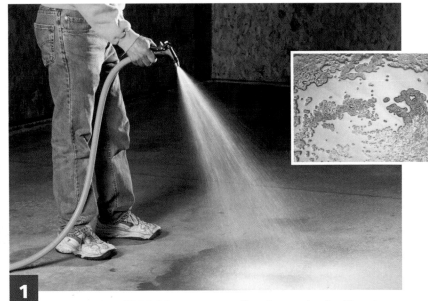

1 **TEST FOR GREASE OR OIL** on a concrete floor by spraying it with water. Beading (inset) shows that oil, grease, or wax are present, any of which will prevent a good bond. Note that a garden sprayer or household spray bottle can be used instead of a garden hose.

CLOSE LOOK

water alert

ANY SIGN OF MOISTURE on masonry floors or walls is a warning. If you notice dampness, efflorescence (white powder), or lifting or blistered paint, there is a water problem. Before you paint, eliminate the water source. If drainage pipes are around your foundation, take these measures:

■ Install roof gutters with downspout extensions to carry rainwater away from the foundation.

■ Slope the ground away from the house.

■ Install a sump pump in the basement to remove water from under the slab.

2 **TEST FOR MOISTURE IN OR UNDER** the slab by taping a 4x4-foot poly sheet over the floor for 24 hours. If the poly sheet is damp or wet, do not paint or stain.

BUYER'S GUIDE

use the right stuff

NEVER USE FLOOR PAINT or ordinary epoxy on a garage floor: Hot tires will stick to it and lift it. Instead, use a paint or stain formulated to withstand hot-tire pickup, such as one-part epoxy, acrylic garage floor paint. Two-part epoxy is also available for particularly tough jobs. Never apply more than two coats of any paint to a garage floor.

3 **IF THE SLAB BEADED IN STEP 1,** scrub with a TSP solution, rinse, and test again. If it still beads, scrub with a degreaser/concrete cleaner.

4 **ETCH THE CONCRETE** with a solution recommended by the manufacturer of the paint you've chosen for the floor. Follow their safety recommendations carefully.

5 **IT IS VERY IMPORTANT TO RINSE** any cleaners and acids from the slab before painting. Otherwise, they may react with the paint or stain, or interfere with paint adhesion.

6 **APPLY A CONCRETE STAIN** or concrete paint using a 9-inch roller cover with a ⅜-inch nap. Figure 250 square feet with the first coat and 400 to 600 square feet with the second. Don't apply more than two coats.

ROOM PAINTING BASICS

99

PAINTING BRICK

Revitalize a brick wall or fireplace with a fresh coat of paint. Follow these steps for success.

STUFF YOU'LL NEED

TOOLS: Chalkline, carbide scorer (or utility knife with plenty of replacement blades), mixing paddle, ¼×¼-inch square-edge trowel, 1-inch brush, roller cover with 1-inch nap, safety goggles, rubber gloves, synthetic brush, wire brush, TSP solution, painter's tape

MATERIALS: Thin-set mortar with acrylic latex admix, primer, flat acrylic latex paint

WHETHER YOUR AIM IS A CHANGE in decor or the preservation of a crumbling surface, painting a brick surface presents unusual challenges and requires painstaking preparation.

As with all painting projects, perfection begins with a clean surface. In addition to dirt and grime, creosote or gas also coats some brick surfaces. And brick often offers the challenge of crumbling mortar, which is devastating to a finish coat of paint.

With brick surfaces, you will invest a lot of elbow grease in surface preparation. To make that investment pay off, allow the surface ample drying time between steps. It is equally important to use quality tools and materials, and to wear proper safety gear.

Repairing but not repainting? Loose, crumbling mortar needs to be removed and replaced even if you're not repainting. Before you apply new thin-set mortar, coat the brick surface with an oil-based sealer. This will help prevent the new mortar from adhering to the brick surface.

1 **IF THERE IS ANY CREOSOTE** on the wall, remove it with a concrete and masonry cleaner. Wear safety goggles and rubber gloves; use a synthetic brush. As you work, you will begin the process of removing crumbling mortar from the joints.

2 **REMOVE LOOSE MORTAR** and that which is adjacent to avoid future crumbling. Use a wire brush the same width as the mortar joint. Wear goggles and protective gloves.

CLOSE LOOK

problem areas

CHISEL OUT MORTAR in joints that are seriously deteriorated. Using a carbide scorer (or a utility knife), gently tap the mortar to loosen it. Clean the surface with a TSP solution, rinse it thoroughly, and give it ample drying time. Apply new mortar, brushing wet mortar off the brick faces as you go.

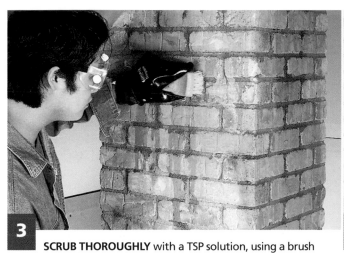

3 **SCRUB THOROUGHLY** with a TSP solution, using a brush with firm, synthetic bristles. Wear goggles and protective gloves.

4 **RINSE AND RINSE AGAIN.** Allow the surface to dry thoroughly. TSP is a suds-free cleanser; you may not see the residue, but it will interfere with adhesion. Rinse at least twice.

5 **REPAIR JOINTS** with thin-set mortar using a square-edge trowel. Brush wet mortar off bricks as you go. For a finished edge, smooth joints and corners. Allow to dry completely.

6 **MASK ADJACENT** surfaces using painter's tape. Use plastic sheets to keep paint spatter off adjacent surfaces.

7 **APPLY A QUALITY LATEX PRIMER** specially formulated for brick, masonry, and stucco, followed by a quality semigloss or gloss latex paint. Use a roller cover with a 1-inch nap.

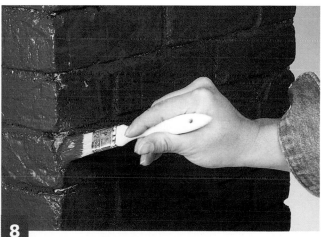

8 **TOUCH UP CORNERS, CRACKS, AND CREVICES** using a 1-inch brush.

INTERIOR PAINT FAILURES

Recognize the source of a problem and you can fix it. Anticipate the problem and you can avoid it entirely.

POOR PERFORMANCE of an interior paint is almost always the result of one of five factors:

- Failure to properly prepare the painted surface.
- Use of inferior or improper applicators.
- Use of low-quality paint.
- Excessive thinning of the paint.
- Painting under improper conditions of temperature or humidity.

CAUSES AND REMEDIES OF INTERIOR PAINT FAILURES

PROBLEM	DESCRIPTION	CAUSE	REMEDY
POOR HIDING	Paint does not completely cover the surface, so a "ghost" of the prior finish shows through.	■ Paint is spread too thin or thinned too much. ■ The method of application does not work well for this paint and substrate. ■ There is a big contrast between new and existing paint colors, especially light over dark. ■ Certain colors don't hide well, such as bright yellows.	■ Don't thin and apply at the recommended spread rate. ■ Use proper application tools (rollers don't hide as well as a brush or spray). ■ If rolling, use a ¼-inch nap for smooth surfaces and a long nap (½ inch or longer) for rough surfaces.
POOR BLOCK RESISTANCE	Surfaces painted with the same paint tend to stick together, such as a door against a door jamb.	■ Paint has not been allowed to dry adequately before being put into service. ■ Dark tints can take longer to dry. ■ High humidity and temperatures increase blocking in latex paints; semigloss blocks more than flat or satin.	■ Allow paint to dry thoroughly before putting into service. ■ If blocking still occurs, apply some talcum powder to both surfaces. Or rub the surface with waxed paper.
SPATTERING	Droplets of paint fly off the roller as paint is applied to wall or ceiling.	■ Paint has been thickened with older-type thickeners, which tend to spatter far more than do those with synthetic thickeners. ■ Wrong size roller nap. ■ The paint has been rolled on too quickly.	■ Use spatter-resistant wall and ceiling paints. ■ Use a quality roller cover with recommended nap. ■ Roll slowly with a short-napped roller.
POOR STAIN RESISTANCE	Common stains tend to be absorbed by the paint and are difficult to remove.	■ Economy flat paint was used or paint was applied at very low temperature.	■ Apply paint under recommended conditions. ■ Priming or second coating can minimize porosity. ■ Remove stains and dirt as soon as possible. ■ Use detergent (not plain water) for cleaning.

PROBLEM	DESCRIPTION	CAUSE	REMEDY
BURNISHING	Painted surface becomes shiny when cleaned or rubbed by furniture.	■ Harsh, abrasive cleaner was used. ■ Some flat paints will burnish. Satin and semigloss are less likely to burnish but will dull with harsh cleaning or repetitive rubbing.	■ Do not use harsh cleaners. ■ Do not use a stiff scrubbing brush. ■ Use a higher-quality flat paint or repaint with a satin or semigloss paint.
MILDEW	Gray, black, or brown fungus on the paint. It can be uniform or spotty in appearance, or both.	■ Fungus may grow on the paint surface where conditions are dark and moist (such as over shower stalls and in laundry rooms).	■ Remove surface mildew before painting. Treat with 1:3 mix of household bleach and water (protect eyes and skin). Leave on 20 minutes (add more as it dries). Scrub off and rinse. ■ Use a quality primer. ■ Apply two coats of quality satin, semigloss, or gloss paint with mildewcide.
POOR TOUCH-UP	The same paint reapplied to a spot looks different than the original in color or sheen.	■ Original surface was porous compared to the painted area that was touched up. ■ Temperature differential between original painting and touch-up painting. ■ Poor color acceptance is evident with brush (darker) vs. roll (lighter) application.	■ Prime before painting. ■ Apply a second coat rather than touch up. ■ Touch-up paint must be properly tinted. ■ Touch up in similar conditions to original job. ■ Flats and low-VOC paints can have the best touch-up.
POOR WASHABILITY	Stains do not wash off readily; paint may be damaged by the cleaning necessary to remove dirt and stains.	■ Use of an excessively strong cleaner or too stiff a scrubbing brush, pad, etc. ■ Economy flat paint was used, or paint was applied at very low temperature. ■ Paint was spread too thin or paint was thinned excessively.	■ Use a high-quality paint. If a flat finish is desired, consider using a satin sheen. ■ Use appropriate cleaner. ■ Apply the paint under proper conditions and at the recommended spread rate.
POOR FLOW AND LEVELING	Brush or roller marks are evident in dried paint.	■ Low-quality application equipment (brush or roller cover). ■ The surface painted was porous. ■ Paint was spread too thin. ■ Paint has gotten thick from repeated opening/closing. ■ Some economy paints don't flow well.	■ In severe cases, sand surface before repainting. ■ Apply appropriate primer; use quality tools and paint. ■ Follow manufacturer's instructions for proper coverage (square feet per gallon). ■ Thin paint if it has become too thick from evaporation.

DECORATIVE PAINTING TECHNIQUES

IN THIS SECTION: add dimension

DECORATIVE FINISHES ADD DIMENSION AND PERSONALITY to any room. So when you've perfected brushing and rolling techniques, add a glaze, stencil, or texture. You'll be amazed at the difference!

In this chapter, you'll find instructions for 20 decorative painting techniques, as well as tips for success.

EVERY ACCESSORY IN A ROOM contributes to a successful color scheme. The color wheel will help you pick combinations that will work together.

DECORATIVE PAINTING PREP

Faux techniques require proper preparation to get great results.

NO AMOUNT OF PAINT, no matter how high its quality, will cover flaws in the wall beneath. Thus, proper preparation, whether for a single coat of paint or decorative painting, is the most important step of any painting project. Don't cut corners—if you don't do it right the first time, you'll do it over again.

STUFF YOU'LL NEED

TOOLS: Utility knife, sponge, rubber gloves, 4-foot stepladder, putty knife, sanding block, paint stirrer, 9-inch roller cage, dust mask, bucket

MATERIALS: 12-inch baseboard masking, 2-inch blue painter's masking tape, drop cloth, TSP solution, crack filler or joint compound, primer, 220-grit sandpaper

1 **REMOVE ALL FURNITURE** or put it in the center of the room. Cover the entire floor and all furniture with drop cloths.

2 **MASK SURFACES NOT TO BE PAINTED.** Overlap the drop cloth with 12-inch baseboard masking.
WASH THE WALL with a TSP solution. Rinse thoroughly with fresh water.

CLOSER LOOK

fantastic masking

WHAT A GREAT INVENTION!
Baseboard masking is attached with blue painter's masking tape and drapes over a drop cloth to protect the floor.

3 **REPAIR SMALL CRACKS** and holes with a small putty knife and drywall joint compound or crack filler.
AFTER THE FILLER DRIES, sand the entire wall lightly using a sanding block with 220-grit sandpaper to remove bumps.

4 **PRIME THE WALL** with a quality latex primer. Depending on the finish color, you may want to tint the primer.
SAND THE PRIMED WALL LIGHTLY with 220-grit sandpaper. A drywall sanding pad speeds the job.

Decorative painting techniques use coats of glaze to add translucency and depth to the finished wall.

GLAZE USED FOR FAUX PAINTING is a neutral paint formula to which no pigment has been added. For most faux finishes, it is mixed with paint to provide transparency and time to apply and work with the faux effect. The glaze is latex based, available in paint departments. Although it looks milky when first opened, it is semitransparent when dry.

Mixing glaze. Manufacturers usually recommend mixing one part paint with four parts glaze, but you can mix it to suit your own needs. Experiment to see what works best for you. Prime and paint a sample board with the base coat you're going to be using.

Test and practice. After the base color has dried, mix paint and glaze in varying proportions, and apply them to see how each looks over the base coat. To get a range of effects, make three paint/glaze mixtures in small disposable cups: one that is one part paint to eight parts glaze, another that is one part paint to four parts glaze, and a third that is equal parts paint and glaze. Try them to determine what you want, or try additional ratios to achieve the look you want. When you find the magic ratio, write it down, in order to duplicate it if the room requires more than one batch of glaze.

Glaze coverage. The amount of glaze used (coverage) depends on the application technique. When the effect is created by applying and then removing glaze, the expected coverage is roughly the same as that of a regular interior latex paint top coat: 400 square feet per gallon. When the effect is created by selectively adding a partial coat of glaze, the coverage may be doubled or more (you'll use half the paint or less).

 **WORK SMARTER**

the right sheen

FOR THE MOST DEPTH AND TRANSLUCENCY, professionals recommend using base coats with finishes that range from satin to semigloss. Flat paint doesn't have the oomph to give you the depth needed to bring painting effects to life.

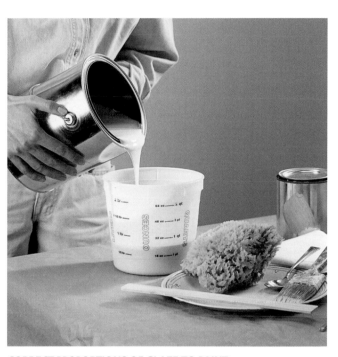

CORRECT PROPORTIONS OF GLAZE TO PAINT are very important especially if you need to mix more to finish the job. Measure carefully and keep a written record.

 **CLOSER LOOK**

mixing custom glazes

ONCE YOU'RE FAMILIAR with faux techniques, you can try mixing your own glazes for special effects. The products can be purchased at paint centers.
The basic formula is:

■ 1 part acrylic latex paint.
■ 1 part acrylic glazing liquid.
■ 1 part water.
■ 2 ounces/gallon gel retarder.

To dilute the effect, or color intensity, of the glaze, add more glazing liquid. To thin the consistency for easier application, add water. To extend the drying time, add gel retarder.

SPONGING ON

Sponge on a glaze for a glimmer of color. You'll add texture, depth, and personality to any room.

SPONGING ON IS THE TECHNIQUE of applying different color paints to a uniform-color base coat. Sponging adds depth to a wall. The more colors sponged on over the base coat, the greater the depth. Glaze coats allow the base paint to show through and extend the drying time of the sponged-on color, giving you more time to work with the effect.

A satin or semigloss base coat is applied with a brush, pad, or roller. The glaze is applied over the base coat with a sea sponge.

Practice, practice, practice. The only way to get comfortable with decorative techniques is to practice on sample boards until you've mastered the technique. The more you practice and experiment, the more color combinations you can try. In the beginning, however, limit yourself to one or two until you get the hang of it.

PAINT CHIP COLORS: (below, left) **A)** Base coat: Moroccan Leather. Glaze: Opera House. **B)** Base coat: Chocolate Mousse. Glaze: Nantucket Shingle. **C)** Base coat: Lodestar. Glaze: Springvale.

STUFF YOU'LL NEED

TOOLS: Utility knife, scrubbing sponge, bucket, rubber gloves, 4-foot stepladder, putty knife, sanding block, dust mask, paint stirrer, 9-inch roller cage with extension handle, roller tray, sea sponge

MATERIALS: 12-inch baseboard masking, blue painter's masking tape, drop cloth, TSP solution, crack filler or joint compound, primer, 3/8-inch nap roller cover, 220-grit sandpaper, clean cotton rags, glazing liquid, acrylic latex paint(s)

A

B   C

Preparing the base. The base for this decorative painting technique is a smooth, freshly painted wall. There aren't any shortcuts worth taking when it comes to preparing a wall for painting. No paint will cover surface flaws, nor will it stick to a wall that is dusty or greasy. So repair and clean the wall first.

Apply primer even if there is already a finish coat of paint on the wall. Primers are specifically designed to stick to the wall and provide the ideal base for a new coat of paint or wallpaper.

Don't scrimp on taping the room. Painter's masking tape is formulated to leave no residue for up to a week. And it's fairly inexpensive when compared to the cost in time of cleaning up paint splatters.

1 **CLEAN AND PRIME THE WALL.** If you don't prime the wall, wash it with a TSP solution. Rinse with fresh water to remove all traces of detergent.

2 **APPLY THE BASE COAT.** Satin or semigloss paints allow a longer working time for the glaze than flat or eggshell. Allow the base coat to dry for 24 hours.

3 **MIX THE GLAZE AS SHOWN** in a ratio of 1 part paint and 4 parts glaze. Practice on test panels to determine the recipe.

 WORK SMARTER

picking color combinations

HIGH COLOR CONTRAST between the base coat and the glaze coats (black and white, for instance) can create dramatic effects. But more subtle gradations in color are easier to live with. Painters recommend using color chips to make selections. Pick a base color on the chip and then choose a glaze color that is two or three gradients above or below it on the chip.

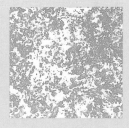

SPONGING ON (continued)

Begin the application. Before sponging the wall, prime the sponge by wetting it under the tap and squeezing out as much water as possible. This will allow the sponge to absorb a full load of glaze.

Next, pour a small amount of mixed glaze onto a ceramic or plastic plate that you can place on a stepladder shelf or carry in your hand. Dip the sponge in the mixture, blot it, and start dabbing.

Be conservative when you start. You can return and sponge on more glaze later—even after the first application has dried. If you sponge on too much glaze in a spot, sponge over it with the base color.

Add more colors. This technique offers a wonderful opportunity to use the color wheel in selecting color.

Start, for instance, with a monochromatic scheme. Enhance that scheme by sponging on a different tint or shade of the base color.

To add a gentle depth, sponge on an analogous color. To make a bolder statement, sponge on a complementary hue. To generate subtle excitement, sponge on colors that form a triad on the color wheel.

If you add a color that you don't like, sponge over it with another color. That's the beauty of painting: A fix is just a brush (or a sponge) away.

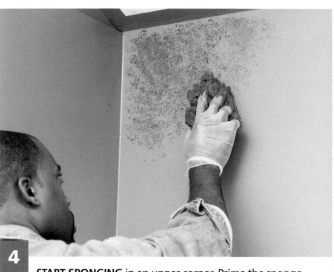

4 **START SPONGING** in an upper corner. Prime the sponge with water and squeeze out the excess. Tear off a small piece of sponge to reach inside corners. Be fluid and rotate the sponge.

5 **SPONGE FROM THE TOP** to the bottom of the wall in a strip as wide as your arm is long.

6 **SWING YOUR ARM IN A RADIUS,** not in a square pattern. Rotate the sponge occasionally.

7 **CARRY A CLEAN RAG** in your other hand, and blot the sponge before starting each new section.

DECORATIVE PAINTING TECHNIQUES

8 STEP BACK AND LOOK at the result after each section. If you need to add more glaze, this is the time to do it.

9 IF YOU SEE A SPOT with too much glaze, go back after the glaze dries and sponge on more base.

10 AFTER THE PREVIOUS glaze color dries, sponge on subsequent color(s), if any.

DECORATIVE PAINT FILE

how to get the look

Sponge on a different tint or shade of the same hue used for the base coat. This will give the walls the look of texture and depth while creating an aura of serenity.

QUICK TIP Avoid repetition by rotating the sponge and flexing your wrist as you sponge. If you're right-handed try sponging with your left. Some painters even sponge with both hands. The first rule is that there aren't any rules.

GOOD IDEA

why sponge on?

If you want the base coat to be the dominant color on the wall sponging on is the way to go. If you want less of the base color to show, use the sponging off technique (page 112).

DECORATIVE PAINTING TECHNIQUES

SPONGING OFF

When you want only a hint of the base coat to shine through, roll on and then sponge off the glaze.

STUFF YOU'LL NEED

TOOLS: Utility knife, scrubbing sponge, bucket, rubber gloves, 4-foot stepladder, putty knife, sanding block, paint stirrer, 9-inch roller cage with extension handle, roller tray, dust mask, sea sponge

MATERIALS: 12-inch baseboard masking, 2-inch blue painter's masking tape, drop cloth, TSP solution, crack filler or joint compound, primer, 3/8-inch nap roller cover, 220-grit sandpaper, clean cotton rags, glazing liquid, acrylic latex paints

SPONGING OFF INVOLVES laying down a solid-color base coat and letting it dry, then rolling on a layer of glaze and blotting with a dry sponge to remove some of the glaze.

This technique gives the wall depth and complexity. The greater the distance on the color wheel between base and glaze colors, the more striking the effect. However, you may want the effect to be quiet and subtle. In that case, use colors closer together on the color wheel. Experiment until you discover the desired level of contrast.

The base coat can be of any sheen and is applied with a brush, pad, or roller. The higher the gloss of the decorative coat, the longer you will have to work with the glaze. Apply the glaze with a genuine sea sponge for the most diverse and interesting result.

PAINT CHIP COLORS: (below, left) **A)** Base coat: Buttercream. Glaze: Yellow Ware. **B)** Base coat: Green Gables. Glaze: Gateway. **C)** Base coat: Meyer Lemon. Glaze: Zesty Orange.

A

B   C

Preparing the base. Sponging techniques give texture to a wall. However, they do not eliminate the need for proper room preparation.

Remove the furniture or group it together in the center of the room. Protect floors and furniture with a drop cloth.

Repair cracks, dents, and mars (pages 56–63). If there are stains on the wall, discover and eliminate their source. Then scrub the wall with a TSP solution. Rinse thoroughly because TSP residue will prevent even the best primer from adhering.

Mask off the room with painter's masking tape. Apply a primer even if there is a finish coat of paint on the wall. Primers provide the ideal base for a new coat of paint and decorative glazing.

1 PREPARE THE WALL by scrubbing thoroughly, repairing surface mars, masking adjacent surfaces, and priming.

2 APPLY THE BASE COAT with a 9-inch roller cover with a ⅜-inch nap. Allow the base coat to dry 24 hours.

3 MIX THE GLAZE in a ratio of 1 part paint and 4 parts glaze. Practice on test panels to determine the recipe.

DECORATIVE PAINTING TECHNIQUES

GOOD IDEA

sponge off

If you want less of the base color to show through, use the sponge-off technique. This produces texture while leaving most of the glaze on the wall. Only a hint of the base coat shines through. If you want to see more of the base color, sponge on (page 108).

Begin the application. Time is critical in sponging off because you are removing glaze. The process stops when the glaze dries. Practice on sample boards until you are comfortable with the technique and with your pace. Also make sure your glaze recipe allows enough time to work. You can slow drying by adding gel retarder to the glaze.

Before you begin, soak the sponge with water. Squeeze out the excess water so the wetness of the sponge will be consistent from start to finish. This is important in maintaining the same effect from section to section.

Have a pile of clean dry cloths or lint-free paper towels handy to blot the sponge when it loads up with paint. Between sections rinse the sponge in a bucket to remove glaze, which tends to thicken inside the pores.

Carry the plate or bucket of glaze in your other hand, or keep it nearby on a chair or stepladder.

Extend your working time. The glaze may dry faster than you can sponge it off. If so, mist the glaze with a spray bottle of water to reactivate it. If this happens more than once, thin the glaze consistency with a little water or add more gel retarder.

If you find you have removed too much of the glaze in a certain spot, you can come back later and sponge on a little bit more.

4 APPLY THE FIRST GLAZE using a 9-inch roller cover with a ⅜-inch nap. Roll as close to the corner as you can.

5 TEAR OFF A SMALL PIECE of sponge and use it to squeeze the glaze into the corners.

6 ROLL AN AREA OF WALL about 3 feet square—as much as you can sponge off in 10 to 15 minutes.

7 PRESS THE SPONGE ON AND OFF the wall, working from top to bottom. Rotate the sponge frequently.

8 **FOR A RANDOM PATTERN,** move your arm radially rather than working horizontally or vertically.

9 **BLOT THE SPONGE** on a rag occasionally. Rinse out the glaze before starting each new section.

DECORATIVE PAINT FILE

how to get the look

Let glazes enhance the color palette used throughout the room. For example, in this bedroom, glazes match the bedspread. As you can see, the glaze takes on a different look under lamp light.

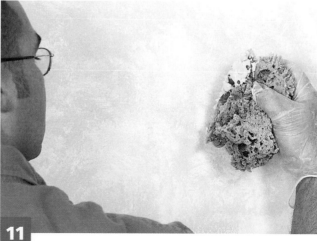

10 **STEP AWAY FROM THE WALL** and look at the result after completing each section.

11 **BEGIN THE NEXT SECTION** before the previous section dries. Always maintain a wet edge.

RAGGING OFF

When you want a diverse texture that helps conceal an uneven surface, use the ragging off technique.

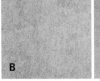

STUFF YOU'LL NEED

TOOLS: Utility knife, scrubbing sponge, bucket, rubber gloves, 4-foot stepladder, putty knife, sanding block, paint stirrer, 9-inch roller cage with extension handle, dust mask

MATERIALS: 12-inch baseboard masking, blue painter's masking tape, drop cloth, TSP solution, crack filler or joint compound, primer, ⅜-inch nap roller cover, 220-grit sandpaper, clean cotton rags, rubber bands, glazing liquid, acrylic latex paint(s)

RAGGING OFF IS SIMILAR to sponging off: You apply a solid-color base coat and allow it to dry, then apply a layer of glaze and remove some of it before it dries. In this case the glaze is removed by rolling a dry, loosely wrapped rag through it. Ragging is a great technique for hiding rough or uneven surfaces, particularly if you use flat paint for both base and glaze.

Ragging off creates various effects, depending on the texture of the fabric and the random wrinkles in the rag. While you can use any clean lint-free cloth, old cotton T-shirts work best. If you don't have an extensive rag or old T-shirt collection, it may be wise to invest in some. You can purchase rags by the pound at most home centers and auto supply stores. Stock up: For this technique, you will need a lot of rags.

When you select your colors, use the color wheel. Colors that are close together on the wheel yield the most subtle effects. Widely spaced colors have more visual impact, but the net effect is more difficult to predict. Practice with sample boards before painting an entire room.

PAINT CHIP COLORS: (below, left) **A)** Base coat: Brass Rail. Glaze: Starlet. **B)** Base coat: Celestial Plume. Glaze: Reverie. **C)** Base coat: Rain Cloud. Glaze: Country Trail.

A

B   C

Preparing the base. Ragging off will help conceal an uneven surface. It will not cover dents, holes, or stains. If there is any mold or mildew on the walls, kill it off by washing with a 1-to-3 solution of bleach and water. Scrub the walls with a TSP solution. Then repair holes, dents, and cracks as shown on pages 56–63.

Use only painter's masking tape for masking. It is formulated to leave no residue for up to one week. Other tapes will stick, but perhaps too well, taking paint with them when they are removed.

Move your furniture from the room or group it together in the center of the room. Cover it with a water-resistant drop cloth.

Wear loose-fitting clothing and a painter's cap—there will be plenty of paint spatters. This technique also generates a lot of slippery paint-soaked rags. Wear shoes with slip-resistant soles and check to be sure the ladder is firmly positioned before you use it.

GOOD IDEA

spray on, rag off

Do you need to touch up a spot after the glaze has become too dry to work? Mist the spot with a spray bottle of water. This reactivates the glaze for touch-up.

If you find that all of the glaze is drying too quickly, add gel retarder to your recipe and remix.

1   **WASH THE WALL WITH A TSP SOLUTION,** then rinse. Mask adjacent surfaces with blue painter's masking tape. Apply the primer recommended by your paint store. Allow to dry thoroughly.

2   **APPLY A SATIN OR SEMIGLOSS BASE COAT** using a roller with a ⅜-inch nap cover. Let the base coat dry for at least 24 hours before applying glaze.

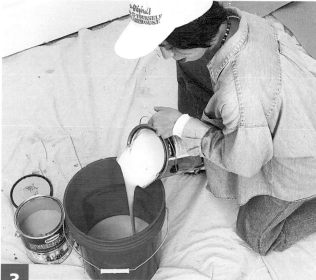

3   **MIX THE GLAZE** in a ratio of 1 part paint to 4 parts glaze. Adjust the color intensity by adding glazing liquid or paint; thin the glaze consistency by adding water.

RAGGING OFF (continued)

The application. Ragging off is the process of removing glaze after it has been rolled on. Timing is critical because once the glaze dries, it can't be removed. That makes practice important for two reasons: You learn the technique and you learn how much area you can rag off before the glaze dries.

It's most efficient to work in areas no more than 10 square feet at a time. This will give you more time to work the glaze before it dries.

Apply the glaze, then start rolling it off at the bottom of each section. The surface of the rag will fill with paint as you work. When the entire surface of the rag is wet, turn it inside out and reroll it. When it becomes wet throughout, replace the rag. Have a partner prepare the rags so you can keep up the pace.

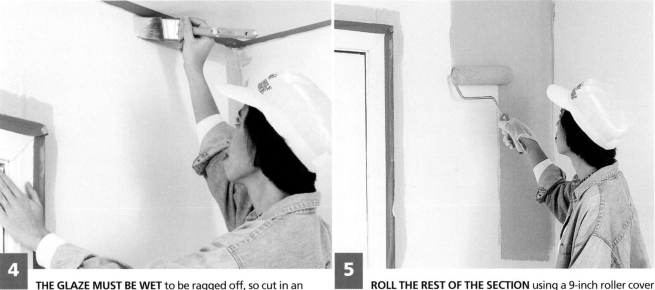

4   **THE GLAZE MUST BE WET** to be ragged off, so cut in an area of no more than 10 square feet using a 2-inch sash brush.

5   **ROLL THE REST OF THE SECTION** using a 9-inch roller cover with a ⅜-inch nap. Work quickly so the glaze doesn't dry.

6   **LOOSELY FOLD (WITH WRINKLES)** a 2×2-foot clean cotton cloth, and roll it into a tube 6 to 8 inches long. Slip rubber bands over the ends to hold its shape.

7   **ROLL THE RAG ACROSS THE WET GLAZE** in random directions until you rag off the entire section. Keep at it until you achieve the effect you want.

8 **CUT IN AND ROLL THE NEXT SECTION** while the first is still wet so that the sections blend seamlessly.

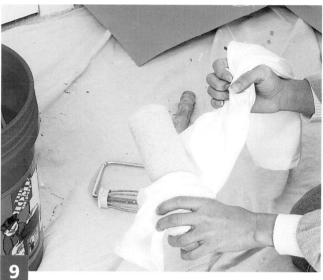

9 **AN ALTERNATIVE TO ROLLING BY HAND** is wrapping the rag around a low-nap roller cover and ragging by rolling. (See page 123 for details on how to wrap the rag on the roller.)

FROTTAGE: USING NEWSPRINT INSTEAD OF RAGS

THE TERM FROTTAGE COMES from the French word *frotter,* meaning to rub. You can rub a newspaper, kraft paper, unprinted newsprint, even plastic. Each material yields a slightly different effect.

Frottage with plastic sacks—also known as bagging—produces a faux leather effect.

The amount of paint left on the wall depends on the consistency of the glaze. Experiment with the wetness of the glaze to vary the amount of ink deposited on the wall.

1. PRESS PAPER INTO THE GLAZE, smooth it with your hands, and let it absorb for a minute.

2. PEEL OFF THE NEWSPAPER. Be careful not to smear the paint, which would ruin the texture.

3. STAND BACK AND OBSERVE THE RESULT. For a stronger effect, leave the paper on longer.

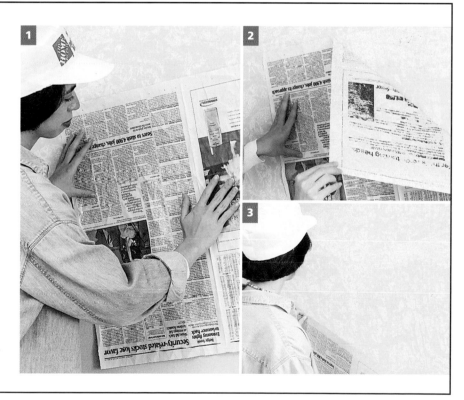

DECORATIVE PAINTING TECHNIQUES

RAGGING ON

When you want to achieve a marbleized effect, use the rag-on technique.

STUFF YOU'LL NEED

TOOLS: Utility knife, scrubbing sponge, bucket, rubber gloves, 4-foot stepladder, putty knife, sanding block, dust mask, paint stirrer, 9-inch roller cage with extension handle, roller tray

MATERIALS: 12-inch baseboard masking, 2-inch painter's masking tape, drop cloth, TSP solution, crack filler or joint compound, primer, ⅜-inch nap roller cover, 220-grit sandpaper, clean 2×2-foot cotton rags, rubber bands, glazing liquid, acrylic latex paint(s)

RAGGING ON IS A TECHNIQUE for adding a nonuniform glaze to a uniform base coat. The base coat and glaze can be two different shades or tints of the same color, or two different colors.

The rag can be either rolled by itself or rolled around a low-nap paint roller cover. The first is the classic technique; the second is simpler and faster.

The rag has to be changed after it becomes saturated with glaze, so you will need several rags. Any cloth will work, but old white cotton T-shirts and cheesecloth are two of the best. Or you can buy rags by the pound at most home centers.

If you have a color combination in mind, paint test panels with one color as the base and the other as the glaze, then the reverse. The results will be quite different.

PAINT CHIP COLORS: (below, left) **A)** Base coat: Pageant Pink. Glaze: Pink Icicle. **B)** Base coat: Ivory Palm. Glaze: Fernette. **C)** Base coat: Monte Carlo Blue. Glaze: Jamaican Blue.

A

B   C

Preparing the base. The base for this decorative finish is a smooth, fresh coat of paint. It's often been said: "A job worth doing is worth doing right." Nowhere is that maxim more true than in painting projects. Professional painters expend most of their effort on prepping: spackling, sanding, cleaning, and priming. No paint, no matter how expensive, will cover surface flaws, nor will it stick to a wall that is dusty or greasy.

Prep your wall. Don't skip any steps: Ragging on is a technique for creating visual depth and texture; it won't hide dents, cracks, or holes.

1 MASK ADJACENT SURFACES and prime the wall with the primer recommended by the paint supplier. Tinting the primer helps the base coat cover better.

2 APPLY THE BASE COAT using a 9-inch roller cover with a ⅜-inch nap. Allow the base coat to dry for 24 hours before applying the glaze.

3 MIX THE GLAZE in a ratio of 1 part paint to 4 parts glaze. If you vary the ratio, record the recipe in case you need to mix more glaze for touch-ups or to finish the job.

GOOD IDEA

primed to rag

Your rag will accept glaze better if you first prime it (dampen it). After wrapping the rag, dip it in a bucket of water, then wring it out and run it over a dry section of the wall, removing the excess water. Run it over a section of wall you plan to rag last, so it will have time to dry before you apply the glaze.

RAGGING ON (continued)

Begin the application. Ragging on is easier than ragging off because there are no time constraints. You can add glaze as much as you want and at any time. If this is your first attempt at using this method, be conservative with the first pass. If you decide the effect is too thin, go back a second time and fill in the gaps.

Eventually the solids in the glaze will build up in the rag, altering the texture. When this happens, throw away the old rag and roll a new one.

If the rags are too large to handle comfortably, cut them into a manageable size before rolling. An alternate to rolling is twisting the rags into a tight spiral. Experiment with both forms.

Color coordination. When you're selecting colors for this technique, use the color wheel. The closer two colors are on the wheel, the gentler the impact on the eye. The farther apart they are, the bolder the result.

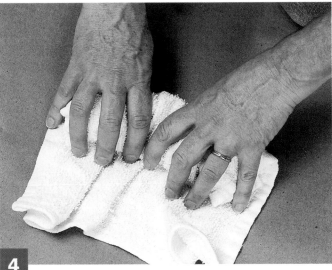

4 FOLD THE CLEAN RAG into a 6-inch-wide rectangle with wrinkles, then roll the rectangle into a loose cylinder. Hold the shape with rubber bands.

5 A DAMP RAG will absorb more of the glaze. Prime it with water, wring it out, then roll the rag in the glaze.

6 STARTING IN A CORNER, roll the wet rag loosely across the wall. Use both hands and roll in random directions rather than vertically or horizontally.

7 STEP BACK TO VIEW the entire wall occasionally to judge the effect. Finish an entire wall before someone else takes over rolling; this will conceal the slight difference in technique.

USING A PAINT ROLLER

YOU CAN SAVE TIME by rolling the rags around a paint-roller cover. The roller has a larger surface, so the rolling goes farther and more quickly. And it's far less messy: Your hands are on the roller handle, not in the glaze.

In the photos below, a 9-inch roller cover with a ⅜-inch nap is used. Experiment with a low-nap cover, such as those used for applying contact cement. For tight areas, use a short, foam hot-dog roller wrapped with a smaller rag. In either instance, you'll need an ample supply of rubber bands to secure the rags to the roller.

WORK SMARTER

change the rag
EVENTUALLY THE RAG will become so soaked with paint that you will begin to lose your pattern. Change it occasionally or move the rubber bands to alter the texture.

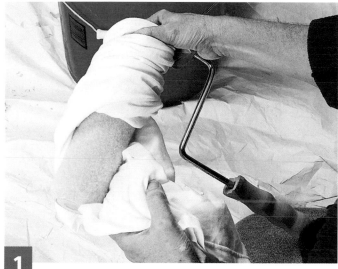

1 **TEAR AN OLD COTTON T-SHIRT** into two rags, then wrap one around a low-nap roller cover, making as many wrinkles as possible.

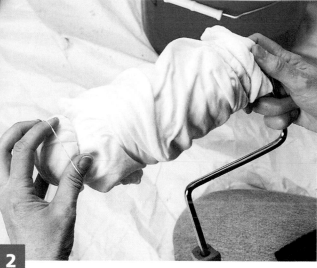

2 **SLIP RUBBER BANDS** over the rolled rag to hold it in place. Narrow bands work better than wide ones. Use a rubber band at each end and one in the middle.

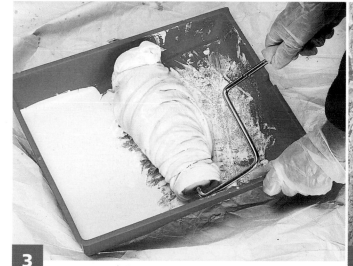

3 **PRIME THE ROLLED RAG** by holding it under running tap water. Squeeze out the excess water and fill the rag by rolling it in a paint tray of glaze.

4 **ROLL THE GLAZE ONTO THE WALL,** starting at an upper corner. Roll in random directions to avoid creating a pattern that is too regular.

COLOR WASHING

To create an aura of antiquity, use a color wash. It's relatively simple and results in an elegant patina.

STUFF YOU'LL NEED

TOOLS: Utility knife, scrubbing sponge, bucket, rubber gloves, 4-foot stepladder, putty knife, sanding block, dust mask, 9-inch roller cage with extension handle, large yellow sponge, 3- and 4-inch brushes, measuring cup

MATERIALS: 12-inch baseboard masking, 2-inch painter's masking tape, drop cloth, TSP solution, crack filler or joint compound, primer, 3/8-inch nap roller cover, 220-grit sandpaper, clean cotton rags, acrylic latex paint(s)

COLOR WASHING can produce a subtle and elegant finish. And it's easy: Casually and lightly brush translucent coats of slightly differing color over a base coat. The effect is a genuine patina of age without the contrived look that is often the result of other forms of antiquing. Color washing works well on textured walls.

You can enhance the effect by using more than one glaze color. Work in a slightly darker shade of glaze around the perimeter of the wall, in the room corners, and on the ceiling.

With color washing, the goal is to make the wall look old. Consequently, there is not as much need to repair surface unevenness or minor blemishes. In fact, you may want to emphasize the rustic look by giving the wall more texture. If so, first skim-coat the wall with plaster (see Fresco, page 166). Then add your color wash.

PAINT CHIP COLORS: (below, left) **A)** Base coat: Chinese Export. Glaze: Kayak. **B)** Base coat: Young Gazelle. Glaze: Windsor Castle. **C)** Base coat: Redware. Glaze: Snowfield.

A

B   C

Preparing the base. To achieve the aura of antiquity with color washing, a certain amount of wall texture is a good thing. Too many dings, dents, and cracks, however, will result in a shabby-looking room.

Prepare your walls carefully. Repair major flaws. Fill in holes and dents. If there is mold or mildew, kill it off by washing with a 3-to-1 solution of water and bleach. Scrub off dirt, grime, and grease. For details, refer to pages 56–63 and 65.

Apply primer even if there is already a finish coat of paint on the wall. Primers are specifically designed to stick to the wall and provide the ideal base for a new coat of paint or wallpaper.

Color wise. When you're mixing colors for your wash, remember that most paint gets darker as it dries and cures.

While you're in the process of repairing, cleaning, and priming the walls, paint test panels with washes of varied intensity. Given a few days to cure, these samples will provide an excellent preview of the color that is to come!

1 **PREPARE THE WALL BY WASHING** with a TSP solution, rinsing, filling holes and dings, sanding, and priming with the product recommended by your paint supplier.

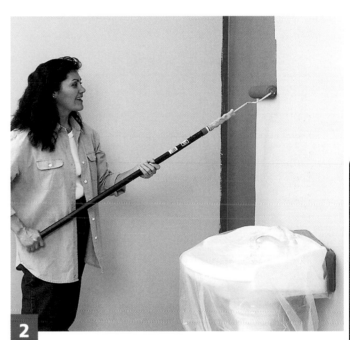

2 **APPLY THE BASE COAT** using a satin acrylic latex paint. Allow the base coat to dry for a minimum of 24 hours before applying the wash.

GOOD IDEA

wash partners

When you're applying a wash, it's good to work with a partner. First, it will speed the job. More important, it will help eliminate any unconscious pattern you might fall into when working alone.

COLOR WASHING (continued)

First technique. Glaze is washed over a darker base coat to introduce a slightly lighter color in this first technique. After the glaze has been applied randomly to a manageable area of wall, the glaze is spread lightly to soften the contrast.

It goes faster if you use a 4-inch paintbrush. You might also use a wallpaper-paste brush. If you find a large brush unwieldy, use a 3-inch brush instead.

A color variation is to apply two glazes: one full strength, the other mixed with an equal amount of white paint. Two glazes results in a more airy, cloudlike effect.

Another variation is to use a darker glaze in the corners, on the ceiling, and around the trim. This will give the room a look of antiquity without making it look like old, grimy paint.

Still another option is to wash on complementary, analogous, or triadic colors. Use the colors on a test panel before you take on an entire wall; you want to achieve the patina of age, not a feeling of chaos!

CLOSER LOOK

tight corners

TO APPLY WASH to inside corners and other close quarters, tear a small piece from a large sponge. Finish the corners while the wall wash is still wet.

3 **MIX THE GLAZE** in at least a ratio of 4 parts glaze to 1 part paint. For more working time increase the ratio. Dip the large sponge into the glaze and wring it out just until it stops dripping.

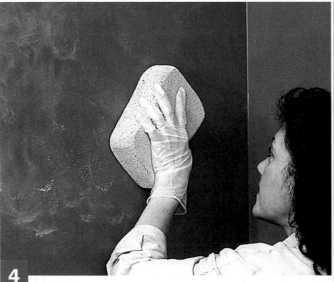

4 **APPLY THE GLAZE** with the wet sponge in 3×3-foot sections, starting at a top corner. Vary the pattern and thickness of the application to emulate the look of natural patina.

5 **BLEND THE GLAZE** with a dry brush. After finishing a section, glaze and brush the next section, blending the wet edges. Periodically clean the brush in water.

Second technique. Applying the glaze is a three-step process in the second technique. First the glaze is rolled onto the base coat in a continuous coat. Next, some of the glaze is ragged off (see Ragging Off, page 118). In the third step of this application process, a second glaze is sponged over the first. Finally the two glazes (washes) are blended to the desired effect with a large paintbrush.

You can take the process to a third level, if you wish, by mixing the first two washes to produce a third wash. Apply this wash with a sponge while the second wash is still wet. Using a paintbrush, blend the washes together to achieve the look you want.

DECORATIVE PAINT FILE

how to get the look

Ragging is a good choice for spaces that get a lot of wear and tear such as children's bedrooms. Coordinate the total color scheme including cabinetry, bed coverings, and furniture. The yellow caution tape allows for a whimsical and personal touch.

1 **APPLY THE WASH TO A 3×3-FOOT SECTION** of wall using a 9-inch roller cover with a ⅜-inch nap rather than a sponge. Cover the surface completely, cutting in as necessary.

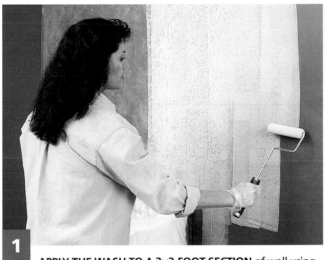

2 **REMOVE SOME OF THE WASH** using the rag-off technique (see page 116). Roll in random directions. Change rags as soon as the rag stops absorbing the wash.

3 **APPLY A THIRD COLOR** (second wash color) with a large sponge, as in the first technique. The first wash should still be wet so the two can blend.

4 **BRUSH THE TWO WASHES** lightly and in all directions, blending the colors to the degree desired. Step back and view your work frequently.

FAUX LEATHER

If your aim is to achieve the look of leather or fine parchment, this is the technique for you.

STUFF YOU'LL NEED

TOOLS: Utility knife, scrubbing sponge, bucket, rubber gloves, stepladder, putty knife, 6-inch knife, sanding block, 4-foot level, measuring tape, 9-inch roller cage with extension handle, dust mask

MATERIALS: 12-inch baseboard masking, 2-inch painter's masking tape, drop cloth, TSP solution, crack filler or joint compound, primer, 3/8-inch nap roller cover, 220-grit sandpaper, clean cotton rags, glazing liquid, acrylic latex paint(s), thin plastic sheeting

DECORATIVE PAINTING TECHNIQUES

FAUX LEATHER TECHNIQUES use plastic bags (or any thin, flexible sheet plastic) to remove wet glaze after it has been applied over a dry base coat of another color. With this technique, you can produce a finish remarkably similar to leather or parchment.

A common faux leather application as shown here is done in panels, making it possible for one person to handle the plastic sheets. Leather doesn't have to be brown. Natural leather is dyed in many colors. Just keep the base coat and glaze close on the color wheel or paint chip.

PAINT CHIP COLORS: (below, left) **A)** Base coat: Gondola. Glaze: Windsor Castle. **B)** Base coat: Bridal Gown. Glaze: Glorious Plum. Glaze: Suave Mauve. **C)** Base coat: Skipping Rocks. Glaze: Snow Day. Glaze: Sneakers.

A

B   C

Preparing the base. The base for faux leather is a clean, smooth wall with a fresh coat of paint. Holes, dents, dings, and cracks will glare through your fine faux finish, ruining the effect.

Thus, it's critical to prepare the walls thoroughly. Wash them to remove dirt, grime, and grease. Repair flaws. And prime the walls with a high-quality primer tinted to match the base coat. For complete details on how to properly prepare a wall, refer to pages 56–63 and 65.

While you're preparing the walls, take the time to hone your skills. Practice on test panels. This will also give you the opportunity to see that the glaze colors are what you have in mind.

Remember that glaze, like paint, darkens as it dries. Use tints and shades that are close to one another on the color wheel to achieve the look of natural leather or fine parchment. As the glaze cures, the difference in hue will become more apparent.

> **GOOD IDEA**
>
> ### planned imperfection
>
> *Leather does have natural imperfections, such as scars where the animal ran into barbed wire or a sharp branch. Use an artist's brush to paint scars on the base coat. Once you have applied a "scar," you won't be able to wipe it up without ruining the mottled effect left by the plastic.*

1   **NATURAL LEATHER HAS A NUMBER OF DEFECTS,** none of which are nail holes or cracks. Prep the wall surface as discussed on pages 56–63.

2   **APPLY THE BASE COAT** of semigloss interior acrylic latex paint. Allow the base coat to dry for at least 24 hours before applying the glaze.

3   **THE PANELS SHOULD BE OF EQUAL WIDTH.** Measure the wall and divide it into equal lengths. Using a 4-foot level, lightly mark the beginning and end of each panel.

FAUX LEATHER (continued)

Begin the application by masking off panels. Masking the panels in a whole wall can be confusing, so get an assistant with whom you can figure the dimensions, and who can stand back and see the whole wall while you apply the tape. One strip of tape on the wrong side of a layout line will throw off the entire pattern.

These photographs demonstrate a light glaze applied over a darker base of the same color. You can also reverse the order, applying a dark glaze over a light base. Experiment to see which produces the most authentic leather look.

Part of the interest of real animal hides is the scars the animal suffered from cuts and scratches.

Experiment by applying thin lines of much darker glaze with an artist's thin watercolor brush before applying the plastic.

CLOSER LOOK

do the whole wall

IF YOU HAVE A HELPER, you can do a whole wall in faux leather. Mix a glaze with a long drying time, apply it to the entire wall, and press a full sheet of plastic onto the glaze. It's just a matter of teamwork and working quickly.

4   **THE PANEL HEIGHTS** should also be equal. Measure the wall, and divide it into equal segments. Mark the horizontal panel dividers with the same 4-foot level.

5   **MASK THE FIRST SET OF PANELS** with 2-inch painter's masking tape applied with one edge along the pencil lines. The panels alternate in a checkerboard pattern.

6   **TEAR THE TAPE AT THE CORNERS** of the panels by ripping it against a 6-inch knife. Or cut the tape using a utility knife and straightedge. (Be careful not to mar the base coat of paint.)

7   **MARK THE PANELS TO BE BAGGED** in the second set with large Xs of painter's masking tape. This will help eliminate any confusion about which panel should be bagged next.

DECORATIVE PAINTING TECHNIQUES

DECORATIVE PAINT FILE

8   **APPLY THE GLAZE** to the first panel using a 9-inch roller cover with a ⅜-inch nap.

how to get the look

Use the faux leather technique to achieve the look of fine parchment. Colors close to each other on the color wheel or on paint chips will provide a subtle and calming finish, but you can also experiment with bolder variations and highly contrasting colors. You can also create interesting effects by applying the glaze coats with a crumpled up plastic shopping bag. Crunch the bag into different shapes and wipe off excess paint as you go.

9   **APPLY 1- TO 2-MIL POLY SHEETING** to the panel and smooth into the glaze. Cut the plastic sheets a little larger than the panels. Press the plastic into the glaze with your hand or a brush.

10   **PEEL THE PLASTIC SHEET OFF** the panel, being careful not to let the plastic slide in the glaze. Clean up messy spots with a sponge or wallpaper brush.

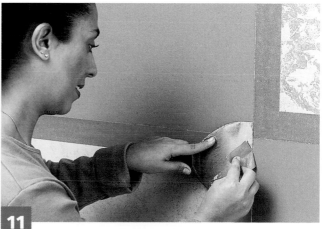

11   **REMOVE THE PAINTER'S MASKING TAPE** immediately. Wait 24 hours for the glaze to dry, then mask the second set of panels in the same way as the first.

DOUBLE ROLLING

You can achieve a subtle yet visually stimulating effect by double rolling and then blending glazes.

STUFF YOU'LL NEED

TOOLS: Utility knife, framing square, tape measure, scrubbing sponge, bucket, rubber gloves, 4-foot stepladder, putty knife, sanding block, double roller with extra covers, double-roller tray, painter's 5-in-1 tool, dust mask

MATERIALS: 4×8-foot sheet of drywall, 12-inch baseboard masking, 2-inch painter's masking tape, drop cloth, TSP solution, crack filler or joint compound, primer, 220-grit sandpaper, clean cotton rags, two acrylic latex paint(s)

DOUBLE ROLLING IS A TECHNIQUE that employs twin rollers to quickly and easily apply a random pattern of two different colors over a uniform base coat. You could use two separate 3-inch rollers and paint trays to achieve the same effect. But that would take twice as much time—or require two people. And the ratios of paints applied would be less uniform.

You will achieve a two-color effect by completely covering the base coat with a twin roller. For a three-color effect, use a different color for the base, and don't completely cover the base coat with the twin rollers.

The effect of double rolling is similar to that of color washing. The benefit is that you have the opportunity to control the degree of subtlety by the amount of final blending and brushing out.

PAINT CHIP COLORS: (below, left) **A)** Base coat: Wheatfield. Glaze: Crepe de Chine. **B)** Base coat: Snow Bell. Glaze: Paris Night. **C)** Base coat: Frosted Pane. Glaze: Green Glade.

A

B

C

DECORATIVE PAINTING TECHNIQUES

MAKING SAMPLE BOARDS

PRACTICE FOR PERFECTION. There are two good reasons the painting pros at The Home Depot advise the use of sample boards: You can learn a technique without ruining a wall, and you can see the actual colors and make adjustments before starting the wall.

1. TO MAKE SAMPLE BOARDS, cut a 4×8-foot sheet of drywall into 2×2-foot squares. To cut the drywall, first score it with a utility knife and then snap it in two.

2. PRACTICE YOUR TECHNIQUE and see the effect of your selected color combinations by double rolling the sample boards.

Preparing the wall. Double rolling produces a mottled finish, but it can't cover defects in the underlying wall. That is why professional painters expend most of their effort on prepping: spackling, sanding, cleaning, and priming. Prep the walls as shown on pages 56–71.

Apply primer even if there is already a new finish coat of paint on the wall. Primers are specifically designed to stick to the wall and provide the ideal base for a new coat of paint or wallpaper.

As you prepare the walls, test your color selection by painting sample boards. Look at the colors in the room you're painting; make your final selection based on the lighting most often used there.

As always, take safety precautions when you're using a ladder (see page 44).

1   **CLEAN AND PRIME THE WALL.** If you don't prime, wash the walls with a TSP solution. Rinse with fresh water to remove all traces of detergent.

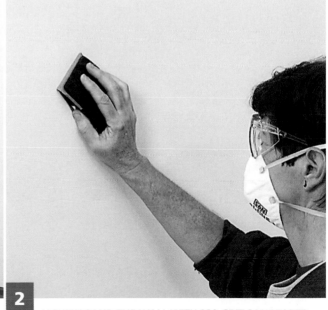

2   **LIGHTLY SAND THE WALL WITH 220-GRIT SANDPAPER** and a sanding block to prepare as smooth a surface as possible. Don't sand through the primer, however. Wipe off the dust.

DOUBLE ROLLING (continued)

The application. Double rolling is nearly as fast as rolling on a single color. The only tricky parts are cutting in to match the random effect and knowing when to stop the blending process. To cut in, first mask the adjacent surfaces with 2-inch painter's masking tape. Then use small (cut off from a large sponge) pieces of sea sponge. Use one for each color, and apply the glaze in alternating dabs.

Knowing when to stop blending is a question of taste, but you should get a feel for it beforehand by rolling several test panels.

You can also double roll with two 4-inch rollers. The one-piece unit has the advantage of ensuring equal applications of the two colors.

A trio of color. This technique actually involves three colors: the base coat plus two shades or tints of

3   **APPLY A BASE COAT** of satin or semigloss sheen. Allow the base coat to dry for at least 24 hours before rolling on the finish.

4   **A DOUBLE ROLLER** requires a matching paint tray with two chambers.

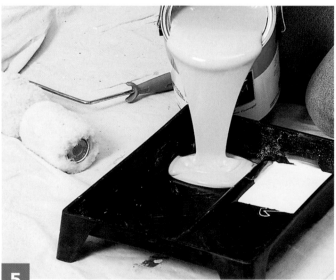

5   **FILL EACH TRAY CHAMBER WITH A DIFFERENT PAINT.** Be careful—if you overfill a chamber, it might spill over into the adjoining chamber when the roller is dipped.

6   **DAMPEN BOTH ROLLER COVERS BY HOLDING** under a tap and squeezing out the excess water. Fill with paint by rolling carefully in the tray.

the same color. The closer the three are on the color wheel, the more subtle the effect. As a general rule, start with your overall color choice, then go two shades darker for one glaze and two tints lighter for the other.

CLOSER LOOK

double roll to death

DOUBLE ROLLING is a technique where you forget everything you've learned about using a roller. In order to get subtle variations in the glaze application, roll, roll, and reroll over the same spot until you get the look you want.

7   **BEGIN ROLLING IN AN UPPER CORNER.** Roll in random directions. Concentrate on getting paint onto the wall rather than covering it completely.

8   **AFTER PAINT HAS BEEN APPLIED LOOSELY** to a 3×4-foot area, continue rolling randomly until the surface is completely covered and the desired effect is achieved.

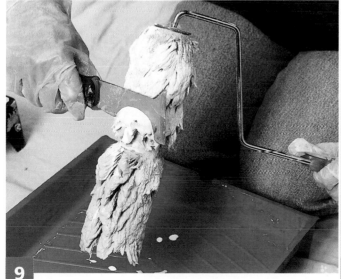

9   **AFTER ROLLING ABOUT FOUR SECTIONS,** scrape the built-up paint from the rollers using the roller-cover scraper on a 5-in-1 tool.

10   **BEFORE IT DRIES,** use several small pieces of sponge to extend the glazes into corners and crevices.

DECORATIVE PAINTING TECHNIQUES

STENCILING BORDERS

Whether you want to emphasize an edge or emulate wallpaper, stencils provide the solution.

STENCILING IS ONE of the oldest techniques for decorating walls. Before the mid-1800s, stenciling was actually less expensive than wallpaper. Stenciling has returned largely because it is such an enjoyable project. And when you need a change, stencils are easier to prime and paint over than a wallpaper border is to remove.

You can buy precut stencils complete with instructions and registration marks, or make your own. Stencil in a single color, or employ colors as you wish. When using multiple stencils, match the registration marks carefully.

PAINT CHIP COLORS: (below, left) **A)** Base coat: Starlet. Stencil: Wild Ivy, Dark Sapphire, Kiwi Green, Berry Red. **B)** Base coat: Oceantide. Stencil: Phthalo Green, Black, Barn Red, Antique Gold, Light Ivory, Sunbright Yellow. **C)** Base coat: Buttercream Frosting. Stencil: Phthalo Green, Ultra Blue, Liberty Blue, Black, Barn Red, Antique Gold, Sunbright Yellow, Dusty Mauve. **D and E)** Base coat: Brass Rail. Stencil: Phthalo Green, Bright Red, Light Ivory, Barn Red, Antique Gold.

STUFF YOU'LL NEED

TOOLS: Plastic scrub pad, rubber gloves, putty knife, 4×7-inch paint pad, sanding block, pencil, ruler or yardstick, fine tapered crafts knife, photocopier, stenciling brushes

MATERIALS: 12-inch baseboard masking, 2-inch painter's masking tape, TSP solution, crack filler or joint compound, primer, 220-grit sandpaper, clean cotton rags, stencil pattern, transparency sheets for photocopier, spray adhesive artist's acrylic paint(s), clear sealer

A

B

C

D

E

Making stencils. If you can't find a ready-made pattern that pleases you, try making your own stencil. Study a ready-made pattern to see how the outline is cut for various effects, then find a pattern or design you like. Make sure, however, that the pattern is not under copyright and is free for use. Copy it to transparency film at a copy center. Cut out the pattern carefully with a fine tapered crafts knife over a piece of poster board.

1 **FIND A PATTERN YOU LIKE** and that is free from copyright restrictions.

2 **ADJUST THE PATTERN SIZE** on a photocopier; add registration marks to the final image.

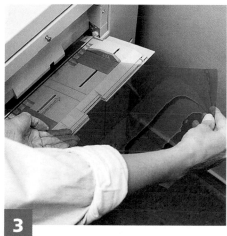

3 **MAKE MULTIPLE TRANSPARENCY COPIES** using transparency film from an office supply store.

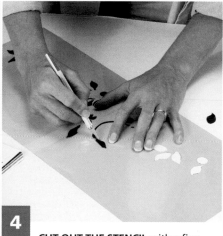

4 **CUT OUT THE STENCIL** with a fine tapered crafts knife. Protect the table top with poster board.

5 **FOR MULTIPLE COLORS,** make several stencils, each with a different part of the design cut out.

6 **SPRAY THE BACK OF THE STENCIL** with adhesive, and test your pattern on poster board.

GOOD IDEA

don't cut corners

If your stenciling will run around one or more corners, be sure to make extra copies. In turning a corner, you will have to either cut the stencil in two or fold it sharply. Both techniques ruin the stencil for straight work. Extra copies will also allow you to continue working when a stencil becomes too built-up with paint.

STENCILING BORDERS (continued)

Applying the stencil. If you buy a stencil, it probably will have a suggested palette of colors. These colors may or may not work with your overall room color scheme, however. Artist's colors are inexpensive in small quantities, so test various color combinations on sample boards. Tape the stenciled boards to the wall so you can see them from a distance and in the room lighting conditions that will prevail.

Another preliminary step that will take a little time, but will make a big difference in the end, is to make enough photocopies of the stencil—make sure there are no copyright restrictions on its use—to cover the entire length and tape them in place. This will show you exactly where the corners fall. Knowing this, you will be able to shift your starting point for the best overall appearance.

Think creatively. This example uses a border stencil along a countertop. Stencils can enhance the decor of any room. Furthermore, you can apply a stenciled border at any height: along the ceiling, at chair-rail height, or along the baseboard. Stencils can also be around a window or door casing.

Stenciling is not limited to borders. Use stencils to create the illusion of wallpaper. Then combine the wallpaper effect with a border stencil.

Have fun!

1   **SCRUB WITH A TSP SOLUTION** to remove dirt and grease. Rinse thoroughly with fresh water to remove all residue.

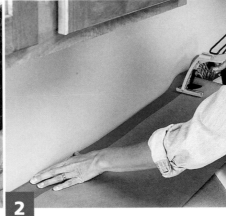

2   **MASK THE AREA** beneath the wall where the stencil will be applied using painter's masking tape.

3   **APPLY THE BASE COAT**—if there is to be one. Allow the base coat to dry at least 24 hours before beginning to stencil.

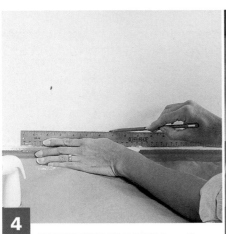

4   **MEASURE UP OR DOWN** from the nearest horizontal surface, and draw a reference baseline lightly in pencil.

5   **PROTECT YOUR WORK SURFACE** with kraft paper, turn the stencil over, and apply spray adhesive to the back side of the stencil.

6   **STARTING AT A CORNER,** position the stencil along the baseline and press it against the wall. Tape the corners with painter's masking tape.

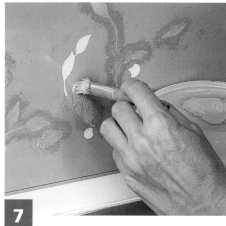

7 **APPLY THE COLORS FOR THE FIRST STENCIL**—here light green that is the base coat for the leaves is stenciled on.

8 **APPLY THE SECOND COLOR.** Dark green is stippled over the base coat to give the leaves shape and texture.

9 **APPLY THE FLOWERS.** Blue is used to fill out the flowers. Before removing the stencil, mark reference points with a sharp pencil.

10 **USING THE REFERENCE MARKS AND THE BASELINE,** shift and tape the first stencil in its next position.

11 **ONCE THE STENCIL IS IN PLACE,** repeat the stencil pattern and order of paint application. Apply the first set of colors again.

12 **AFTER COMPLETING THE ENTIRE LENGTH** with the first stencil, repeat with the second stencil and second set of colors, using the same reference marks for alignment. When the design is dry apply a clear sealer.

GOOD IDEA

keep those stencils clean

If the stencil becomes too built-up with paint, or if you want to save it for another day, scrub it clean with mild detergent and dry on paper towels.

DECORATIVE PAINTING TECHNIQUES

DRAGGING

To achieve the look of fine linen or natural grass paper, use the dragging technique.

DRAGGING IS A SIMPLE TECHNIQUE consisting of nothing more than dragging a dry brush through a wet glaze that has been applied over a base coat of the same or similar color.

You can purchase a special dragging brush or a 3- or 4-inch high-quality brush will work as well.

The technique is simple. But dragging a brush all the way from ceiling to baseboard in one continuous, fairly straight motion can be difficult. Stepping up and down a stepladder for each stroke can be tiring as well. For these reasons you might consider the portion of wall above or below a chair rail for your first dragging project. Or enlist a helper to alternate passes. Taking turns will give you enough time between passes to rest and clean your brush.

PAINT CHIP COLORS: (below, left) **A)** Base coat: Churned Butter. Glaze: Skinned Knee. **B)** Base coat: Whispering Wind. Glaze: Floridian. **C)** Base coat: Ballerina. Glaze: Pageant Pink.

STUFF YOU'LL NEED

TOOLS: Utility knife, scrubbing sponge, bucket, rubber gloves, 4-foot stepladder, putty knife, sanding block, 9-inch roller cage with extension handle, dust mask, edging pad, brush for dragging

MATERIALS: 12-inch baseboard masking, 2-inch painter's masking tape, drop cloth, TSP solution, crack filler or joint compound, primer, 3/8-inch nap roller cover, 220-grit sandpaper, 3/4-inch machine nut, string, clean cotton rags, glazing liquid, acrylic latex paint(s)

A

B

C

DECORATIVE PAINTING TECHNIQUES

Preparing the base. Dragging does not eliminate the need for preparation. Apply a primer even if there is already a finish coat of paint on the wall. Primers stick to the wall and are the ideal base for a new coat of paint.

Before you prime, scrub the wall thoroughly with a TSP solution and repair any holes, dings and dents. Wash any mold or mildew with a 3-to-1 solution of water and bleach. Mask with painter's masking tape, which is less likely to stick to and lift the paint.

Color conscious. If you're going for subtle contrast, use colors that are close to one another on the color wheel. For a more striking effect, use complementary or triadic colors. Remember that most paint darkens as it dries. Before you decide to deepen the contrast, allow the paint to cure for a few days.

1 **DRAGGING REQUIRES A SMOOTH BASE.** Prepare the wall as shown on pages 56–71, applying the primer recommended by your paint supplier.

2 **APPLY A BASE COAT** of acrylic latex satin or semigloss paint. Allow the base coat to dry for at least 48 hours before applying the glaze.

3 **PREPARE THE GLAZE** in a ratio of 1 part satin or semigloss paint to 4 parts glaze. Practice on sample boards until you achieve the dragging effect you're looking for.

DECORATIVE PAINTING TECHNIQUES

GOOD
IDEA

rapid repair

If the effect looks too coarse, you can repair it while the glaze is still wet: Drag the brush through the area a second time. This time, hold the brush nearly perpendicular to the wall and apply less pressure.

DRAGGING (continued)

Preparing to drag. Dragging requires speed and a steady hand. The glaze must be quite wet for the brush to produce the desired effect, and it must remain wet long enough for you to make two or more passes from ceiling to floor.

Keep the lines straight. Plumb bobs hung from the ceiling every 18 inches (see Step 4) can serve as references, keeping you from straying too far from vertical as you drag. You can either tape the plumb bobs to the ceiling or have a helper hold them in place temporarily.

Work with a helper. Dragging is easier with two people. One person rolls the 18-inch strips of glaze; the other person immediately drags the freshly rolled paint. If the glaze dries too quickly, add gel retarder or water.

Do you need special tools? You can purchase special dragging brushes or you can substitute with

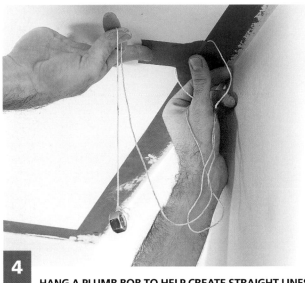

4 **HANG A PLUMB BOB TO HELP CREATE STRAIGHT LINES.** Tie a ½- or ¾-inch machine nut to a string and tape the string to the ceiling, 2 inches out from the wall and 18 inches from the corner, as you would a plumb bob.

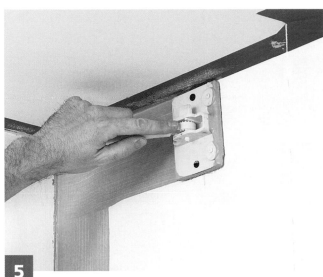

5 **USING AN EDGING PAD,** cut in the glaze in the room corner and 18 inches along the ceiling to the plumb string.

6 **USING A 9-INCH ROLLER COVER** with a ⅜-inch nap, roll the first 18-inch strip of glaze from floor to ceiling.

7 **HOLD THE BRUSH** so that you can maintain the same dragging angle from ceiling to floor without pausing.

something you already own. The dragging brush is wide (to cover ground quickly) and has rather short, stiff bristles. Inexpensive wallpaper brushes and throwaway chip brushes are similar in construction, the first being wider and the second narrower than the dragging brush. Experiment with these before investing in a special, single-use dragging brush.

Differing texture. For a variation on the theme, cut alternating sections of bristles back ¼ inch. The result will be a more interesting banded pattern.

Dragging produces the texture of grass paper or fine linen. Use complementary colors for a strong visual statement. Or use tints and shades of the same color to produce a more subdued effect.

When you're mixing glazes, remember that most paint becomes darker when it is dry.

8   **STARTING AT THE TOP OF THE WALL,** drag the brush vertically from the ceiling to the floor as close as possible to the corner.

9   **AFTER EVERY PASS OF THE BRUSH,** remove the glaze from the bristles by wiping them against a clean cotton cloth or paper towel.

10   **USING THE RIGHT EDGE** of the previous pass as a guide for the left edge of the brush, drag the second strip from ceiling to floor.

11   **A FABRIC EFFECT CAN BE CREATED** by dragging the brush horizontally over the vertically dragged strips. The glaze must still be wet, so move quickly.

COMBING

Create specialized effects such as moiré or basket weave by combing through wet glaze.

STUFF YOU'LL NEED

TOOLS: Scrubbing sponge, bucket, rubber gloves, 4-foot stepladder, putty knife, sanding block, 9-inch roller cage with extension handle, dust mask, utility knife, scissors, squeegee, paint comb(s), tape measure, 4-foot level, 7-foot 1×4 board

MATERIALS: 12-inch baseboard masking, 2-inch painter's masking tape, drop cloth, TSP solution, crack filler or joint compound, primer, ⅜-inch nap roller cover, 220-grit sandpaper, clean cotton rags, glazing liquid, acrylic latex paint(s)

COMBING IS THE DRAGGING OF A COMB through a wet glaze that has been applied over a dry base coat. Prepare the base coat and glaze using different colors, or try different shades or tints of the same color.

Combing can be as simple as a series of straight vertical or horizontal lines. For variety, you can use the comb to create intricate wavy or crosshatched patterns with multiple passes. On the following pages you will find three patterns: straight, moiré, and basket weave.

You can purchase combs with notches of various widths and spacings at paint centers and art supply stores. If you prefer, you can make your own from a window squeegee, as shown on the facing page.

As with the other decorative techniques, practice first on test panels until you achieve the effect you are looking for.

PAINT CHIP COLORS: (below, left) **A)** Base coat: Knoll Green. Glaze: Polynesia. **B)** Base coat: Mud Puddle. Glaze: Pottery. **C)** Base coat: Dapper Tan. Glaze: Blue Angels.

PAINT COMBS: MAKE OR BUY

THE COMB YOU USE determines the effect you achieve. Select one from your local paint center. Or make your own paint comb using any flexible, waterproof material.

PAINT CENTERS CARRY A VARIETY of decorative painting combs. You may want to purchase a few different styles to use on test panels. Then use the one you like best.

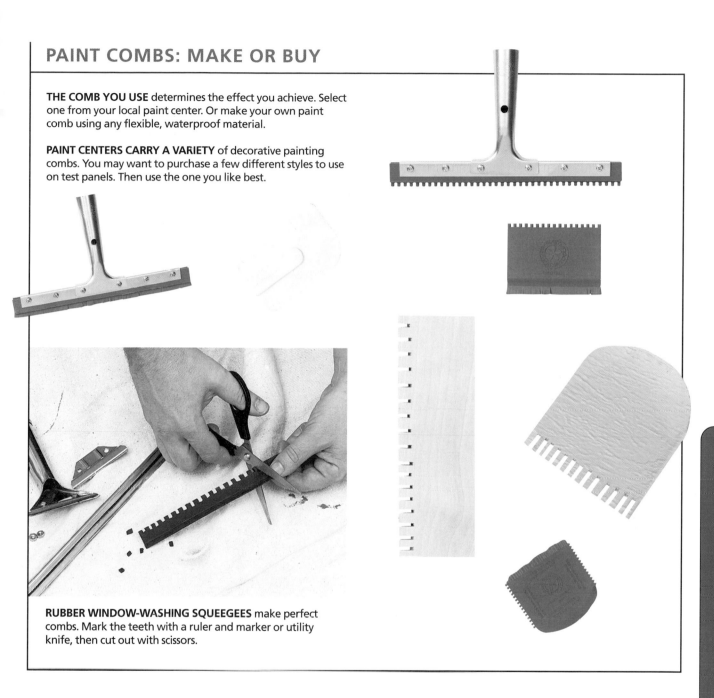

RUBBER WINDOW-WASHING SQUEEGEES make perfect combs. Mark the teeth with a ruler and marker or utility knife, then cut out with scissors.

GOOD IDEA

guidelines

Some decorative techniques require marking the walls with guidelines. Don't use any sort of ink pen or grease pencil because the marks they leave will often bleed through the paint. Instead, use a colored pencil of the same color as the paint; the lines will disappear as you paint over them.

COMBING (continued)

STRAIGHT PATTERN

COMBING IS NOT LIMITED to the uniformly spaced small teeth shown here. Visit a paint center to see the variety of combs available. Combs can be made from rubber squeegees, as shown on the previous page. Another common comb material is a plastic lid from a coffee can.

The comb pattern is not the only variable. Because you are rolling each strip, you can alternate glazes to achieve variation on a much larger scale. Or you can glaze one strip of wall and not the other.

Keeping the comb steady is critical to the end result. A ceiling-to-floor straightedge held along one edge of the comb will allow you to draw perfectly straight lines, but to avoid changes in thickness of the lines, you will have to find a way to drag in a continuous motion.

What happens when you get to the end of the wall and the width of the strip is less than the width of the comb? If you made your own comb, just cut it to the width of the strip, or make another comb from a plastic coffee can lid.

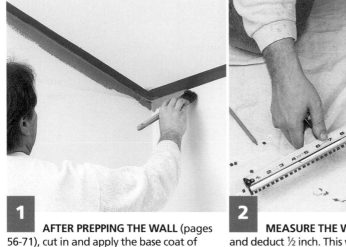

1 **AFTER PREPPING THE WALL** (pages 56-71), cut in and apply the base coat of semigloss acrylic latex interior paint.

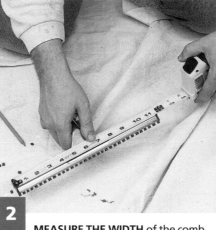

2 **MEASURE THE WIDTH** of the comb and deduct ½ inch. This will be the width of the bands between masking tape strips.

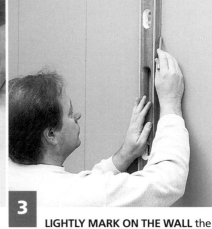

3 **LIGHTLY MARK ON THE WALL** the locations of the vertical strips using a pencil and a 4-foot level.

4 **MASK THE ALTERNATING STRIPS** by aligning one edge of 2-inch painter's masking tape with the pencil lines.

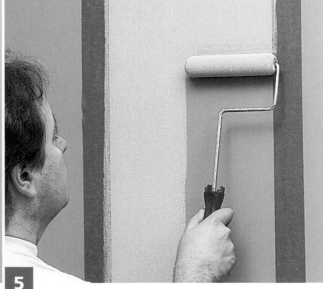

5 **APPLY THE GLAZE** (top coat) to a masked strip using a foam hot dog roller.

Color selection. The color wheel is a useful tool in selecting colors for this technique. The farther apart colors are on the wheel, the stronger the statement.

If you are using one color, select a glaze that is two or three shades darker or tints lighter than the base coat. If you're using more than one color, select colors that are complementary, triadic, or analogous on the color wheel (pages 19–20).

WORK SMARTER

remove the masking tape
DON'T FORGET TO REMOVE THE MASKING TAPE before the paint dries, otherwise you'll pull pieces of your pattern right off the wall.

6   **WITH A PARTNER HOLDING A BOARD** along one edge as a guide, pull the comb from ceiling to floor.

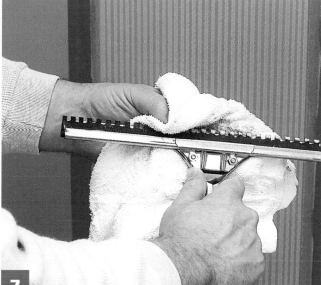

7   **AFTER EACH PASS,** clean the comb of paint with a clean, lint-free, noncolored, absorbent cloth.

8   **APPLY THE GLAZE TO THE SECOND MASKED STRIP,** comb the second strip, clean the comb, and repeat the steps.

9   **AFTER ALL STRIPS HAVE BEEN COMBED,** remove the painter's masking tape before the paint dries.

DECORATIVE PAINTING TECHNIQUES

COMBING (continued)

MOIRÉ PATTERNS

WHEN TWO REGULARLY SPACED PATTERNS overlap but are slightly misaligned, a moiré pattern is produced. The eye detects, in addition to the two different patterns, a third pattern where the first two patterns intersect. Overlapping window screens often produce moiré patterns.

The slighter the misalignment, the larger the moiré pattern. A larger comb spacing also results in a larger moiré pattern.

Moiré patterns create a feeling of dynamic tension. Use them in areas of activity, such as the family room or kitchen. It is best not to use moiré patterns in rooms such as bedrooms, where you want to rest.

1   **MARK THE STRIPS AND APPLY** the painter's masking tape in the same manner as for straight combing (pages 146–147).

2   **CUT IN TOP AND BOTTOM,** then apply the glaze to the first strip with a hot dog roller.

3   **PULL THE COMB THROUGH THE BAND** from ceiling to floor in a continuous sinuous curve. Make sure the comb always covers the entire strip.

4   **CLEAN THE COMB WITH A CLEAN CLOTH,** then pull it through the strip a second time, this time in the mirror image of the first pass.

5 APPLY THE GLAZE to the next 18-inch strip and repeat steps 2 through 4. If the glaze dries too quickly, have a partner glaze while you comb.

6 STEP BACK AND LOOK at the finished product. If you want, you can go back and reglaze and recomb a strip before the glaze dries completely.

7 REMOVE THE PAINTER'S MASKING TAPE before the glaze dries entirely or the tape may lift off some of the paint in a strip.

HORIZONTAL COMBING

COMBING CAN BE A HORIZONTAL, as well as vertical, effect. The only difficulty is in dragging the top strip. Set up a plank and scaffold to walk along.

BASKET-WEAVE PATTERN

BY COMBING SQUARES HORIZONTALLY and vertically, you can create a basket-weave effect. Unlike the moiré pattern on the previous pages, the basket-weave pattern is visually stimulating, but restful.

The basket-weave technique, even when used with a straightedge to guide the comb, has a handmade feeling. This is because the comb fills with paint as it moves, resulting in slight differences in line width, and therefore color, at the beginning and the end of the stroke.

As a general rule, size the comb to the scale of the wall: large wall/wide comb; small wall/narrow comb.

Restful colors. Because this technique creates a restful aura, use it in areas where you want to create a feeling of relaxation.

This does not mean, however, that you should limit your color selections to different tints or shades of the same hue or analogous colors. Areas of relaxation need not be void of visual stimulation! Use test panels to experiment with complementary or triadic color schemes. As you see the color combinations come to life, you'll also gain valuable experience in combing through glaze.

1 **STARTING FROM THE TOP OF THE WALL,** mark the vertical tapes with a black marker in increments of squeegee lengths.

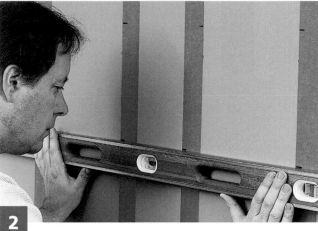

2 **MAKE SURE ALL OF THE CORRESPONDING MARKS** are at the same level. Use a 4-foot level or a pair of helpers and a length of string to ensure linear consistency.

3 **CUT IN THE TOP OF THE FIRST STRIP** with a sash brush, then roll the rest of the strip with glaze using a hot dog roller.

4 **DRAW THE COMB HORIZONTALLY** through the paint between alternating sets of marks. Use a horizontal straightedge for perfectly straight lines.

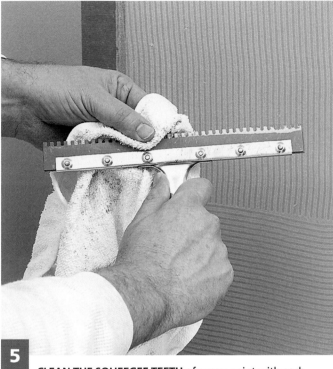

5 **CLEAN THE SQUEEGEE TEETH** of excess paint with each pass to avoid uneven paint ridges.

6 **AFTER ALL OF THE HORIZONTAL SQUARES** have been combed, pull the comb vertically through the alternate squares, one at a time.

7 **REMOVE THE PAINTER'S MASKING TAPE** before the glaze dries completely or the tape may lift off the paint in spots.

8 **THE FINISHED EFFECT IS THAT OF A BASKET WEAVE.** For greater effect, make the base coat and glaze different tints or different colors.

SPATTERING COLORS

Whether you want to simulate stone or impart a feeling of lighthearted joy, spatter colors.

STUFF YOU'LL NEED

TOOLS: Utility knife, scrubbing sponge, bucket, rubber gloves, 4-foot stepladder, putty knife, sanding block, dust mask, 9-inch roller cage with extension handle, 3-inch chip brushes (one for each color), stirring stick

MATERIALS: 12-inch baseboard masking, poly sheeting, 2-inch painter's masking tape, drop cloth, TSP solution, crack filler or joint compound, primer, 3/8-inch nap roller cover, 220-grit sandpaper, clean cotton rags, acrylic latex paint(s)

SPATTERING IS ONE OF THE OLDEST techniques for decorating walls and floors. It involves simply drawing a stick across the bristles of a brush to project a spray of droplets, or paint spatter, onto a wall or floor.

When the base coat and the spatter color are shades and tints of the same color, the effect can be quite subtle, resembling certain natural stones. When the colors are many and sharply contrasting, the effect is like that of confetti, conveying a lighthearted feeling. Decide which effect you wish to create. Then, using the color wheel (pages 16–20), create a palette of several colors to achieve the effect you want.

PAINT CHIP COLORS: (below, left) **A)** Base coat: Hawaiian Waters. Spatters: Silver Springs, Blue Bow, Blackfee. **B)** Base coat: Barrister White. Spatters: Basket Tree, Side Saddle, Stone Grey. **C)** Base coat: Ultra Pure White. Spatters: Epic Blue, Beyond Red, Yellow Cluster, Green Court.

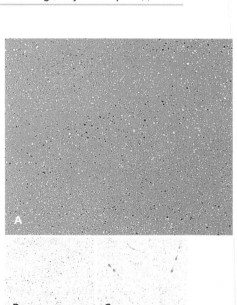

A

B   C

Preparing the base. Don't just start spattering paint on the wall. Paint, no matter how expensive, is a very thin coating. Surface defects in the substrate will probably show through. Nail holes, hairline cracks, crayon marks, even the relatively smoother areas where the drywall was taped, will show through the best base coat.

Professional painters expend most of their effort on prepping: spackling, sanding, cleaning, and priming. Go with the pros; prepare your wall for painting as shown on pages 56-71.

When you're spattering paint, the brush is 18 to 24 inches from the wall. Still, paint spatters fly all over. Be sure to cover all surfaces you want to keep free of spatter.

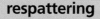

GOOD IDEA

respattering

Unlike other techniques, paint spatters can be added at a later time. Rather than trying to achieve the desired drop density on the first pass, spatter the entire wall lightly. Step back and look at the effect, then come back and add spatter until you have it right. Remember: You can always add drops, but you can't take them back.

1 **AFTER WASHING AND PRIMING THE WALL,** mask all other room surfaces, including the ceiling. Cover doors and windows with poly sheeting. Paint spatters will fly everywhere.

2 **POLY SHEETING IS SLIPPERY UNDERFOOT,** so protect the floor with a paper/poly drop cloth. Tuck the drop cloth under 12-inch baseboard masking for total floor protection.

3 **APPLY THE SATIN OR SEMIGLOSS BASE COAT** using a 9-inch roller cover with a ⅜-inch nap. Allow the base coat to dry for 24 hours before beginning to spatter.

4 **A GOOD STARTING POINT** for the spatter paint is 2 parts acrylic latex paint to 1 part water. Adjust the consistency so the droplets don't run down the wall.

SPATTERING COLORS (continued)

The application. Spattering is, by nature, a random effect. For that reason there is no standard by which to measure your success. If it looks good to you, then it is perfect!

Of all the decorative painting techniques in this book, spattering is most suitable for and within the abilities of children. Spattering a child's room can be an enjoyable experience for the entire family.

Walls aren't the only surfaces you can spatter. Ceilings and floors are also potential canvases. Spattering a ceiling is simpler than spattering a wall. Paint drips on a wall run down the wall and are visible. Drips on a ceiling, on the other hand, simply drop onto the drop cloth on the floor.

Spattering a floor is simplest because you can thin the paint without danger of running. You can

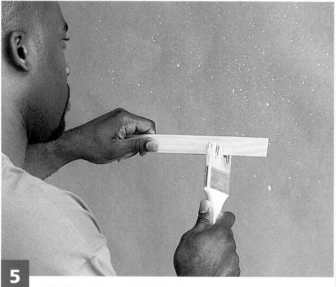

5 **TEST THE PAINT CONSISTENCY** and your spattering technique on kraft paper taped to the wall. Spatter by drawing a paint stirrer across the bristles.

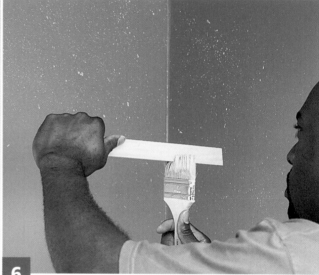

6 **START SPATTERING AT A TOP CORNER** at a distance of 18 to 24 inches from the wall. Droplet size depends on the distance of the brush from the wall, so be consistent.

7 **WORK FROM CEILING TO FLOOR** in a strip about 1 foot wide. Don't overdo the spatters. You can add spatters later, but you'll have to repaint to remove them.

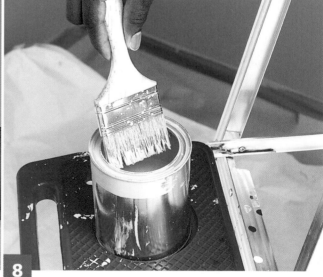

8 **RELOAD THE BRUSH WHEN THE SPATTERS** become too small. Dip the bristles one-third of the way into the paint, and do not wipe the tips on the lip of the can.

produce extra-large drops for a floor by tapping the brush ferrule against your hand or a heavy object such as the head of a hammer. The only problem with a floor is that you have to remember not to walk over a spattered area before it cures.

When you're spattering, be sure to completely protect surfaces you don't want spattered. Time invested in cover-up will be time saved in cleanup.

CLOSER LOOK

spatter machine

A PAINT SPRAYER WITH AN ADJUSTABLE NOZZLE will give you great spatter effects in record time. Sprayers can either be electrically powered or hand-pumped. Clean the sprayer thoroughly between colors.

9   **KEEP YOUR EYES OPEN FOR DRIPS.** Small drips are OK; wipe up large drips immediately with a damp paper towel wrapped around your forefinger.

10   **STAND BACK AND EXAMINE** your work periodically. Be conservative—especially if you will be adding more colors. You can always fill in light spots.

11   **AFTER SPATTERING AT LEAST** one complete wall with the first color, repeat the process with the second color using a clean brush.

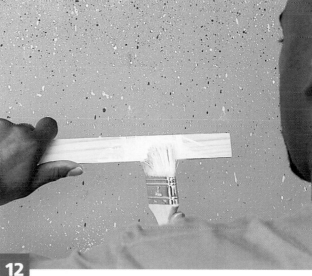

12   **APPLY AS MANY COLORS AS YOU WISH.** You don't have to wait between colors; the droplets dry almost instantly.

DECORATIVE PAINTING TECHNIQUES

FAUX MARBLING

Marble is the aristocrat of natural stone and appropriately expensive. Get the look of marble for the price of a few cans of paint.

STUFF YOU'LL NEED

TOOLS: Level, marking pencil, paint roller, trim roller, tray, plastic drop cloth, stippling brush, feathering brush, synthetic brush for polyurethane, painter's masking tape, turkey feather (for veining)

MATERIALS: Quality latex semigloss paint for base coat, quality latex semigloss paint for second marble color, latex glaze, latex paint for veining

FAUX MARBLING IS AN AFFORDABLE WAY TO CREATE THE LOOK OF FINE STONE. The depth and variety of color in natural marble allows faux painters a great deal of freedom to create looks that range from striking and dramatic to simple and understated. Marble tiles possess many different colors and a variety of combinations embedded in the stone.

The wainscoting treatment shown here creates dark green marble panels set in a green limestone frame. Wainscoting, which refers to the siding on a wagon, was applied to protect walls from everyday wear and tear.

Faux marbling is a simple technique, especially if you practice. The most common method is to sponge on layers of color. The method in this project uses a sheet of plastic—a variation of a classic paper technique called frottage. The directions suggest a couple of variations that add color and depth to the finished look. The frame around the panels has been stippled to resemble limestone, and the wainscoting has been capped with a chair molding.

PAINT CHIP COLORS: (below, left) Base coat: Ink Black. Glaze coat: Woodsman Green. Veining color: White. Stipple base: Fox Hollow. Stipple glaze: Smoky Emerald.

1 APPLY THE BASE COAT AND STIPPLE ON THE GLAZE COAT FOR THE ENTIRE WALL. (See page 162.) Then lay out the marble panels with a pencil and level. The panels shown are 5 inches below the chair rail, 20 inches wide, and 22 inches high, with a 6-inch-wide stile separating them.

After laying out the panels, mask the stiles. Use a low-tack tape around the panel, aligning the inside edge with the outside panel edge.

2 APPLY THE MARBLE BASE COLOR. Marbling begins with a base coat of color that peeks through subsequent coats. Select the color, roll it on the panels, and let it dry thoroughly.

3 MIX AND APPLY THE GLAZE. The glaze mixture applied over the base is 1 part paint to 4 parts glaze. Roll it on only one panel at a time so that the glaze doesn't dry out before you finish working with it.

QUICK TIP Don't get so caught up in your work that you forget to step back to see how you're doing. Looking at the big picture now and then will help you avoid repetition and redundancy.

4 MARBLEIZE THE GLAZE MIXTURE. Use a plastic drop cloth to give the glaze a mottled appearance. Cut the drop cloth about an inch wider and longer than the marble panel. Place the plastic on the wall against the wet glaze, wrinkling it randomly. The wrinkles create sharp lines in the glaze, similar to the color shifts in marble. With your hands, push the plastic against the wall and mush it around to create a mottled marble look. Remove the plastic and discard it. Use fresh plastic for remaining panels.

Faux finishers often add a second or third coat of glaze. To try this, start with the lightest glaze, apply, and mottle it. Let it dry thoroughly. Apply and mottle a darker glaze. Repeat with a slightly darker glaze for a third coat.

5 APPLY THE VEINING. Create the veins with a turkey feather. If you have difficulty locating one, check in a costume shop or a fly-fishing shop. Stroke the feather from tip to tail to create individual clumps of fibers. Dip the feather lightly into the veining paint. Drag the feather along the wall to make thin, meandering lines diagonally across the tile. Twist the feather to vary the width and quality of the veins as you drag the feather along.

Finishers often let the first lines dry, then drag another series of fine lines at diagonals to them. If you do this, don't soften the new lines with a brush as described in the next step. Leave them sharp so they appear to run along the surface, increasing the illusion of translucency.

6 BRUSH OUT THE VEINING. Create the illusion of the vein continuing below the surface. Drag a feathering brush along one side only of a wet line to feather the distinct vein edge.

When the panels are thoroughly dry, tape out the borders that surround them and roll paint onto the border area using a small trim roller. Work carefully to avoid getting paint beyond the masked areas. Remove the masking tape while the paint is still wet.

To protect the finish and increase the effect of depth, allow the marbling to dry thoroughly before applying one or more coats of untinted glaze.

SOUTHWESTERN TEXTURING

When you want to achieve a finish that simulates natural stone, veneer the wall with tinted plaster.

STUFF YOU'LL NEED

TOOLS: Scrubbing sponge, rubber gloves, 4-foot stepladder, plaster trowel, mason's hawk, sanding block, dust mask, spray bottle, plastic auto-body trowel, 5-gallon bucket, ⅜-inch drill and mortar paddle, utility knife, framing square, measuring tape

MATERIALS: 12-inch baseboard masking, 2-inch painter's masking tape, drop cloth, TSP solution, primer, 220-grit sandpaper, dry plaster, tint, clear plaster sealer, drywall, drywall screws

SOUTHWESTERN TEXTURING, also called veneer plastering, produces a shiny, natural stonelike surface most often identified with contemporary Southwestern interiors.

The technique requires two thin applications (⅛ inch) of finishing plaster over an existing painted wall, or a new wall covered with "blueboard" gypsum board or the back side of regular gypsum board.

Each application of plaster must be finished in one operation or the stopping/starting seams will crack. For this reason, and because you have only 45 minutes in which to work a plaster batch, it is advisable to have several helpers—one to mix plaster and the others to apply the plaster.

Screw several 4×8-foot sheets of drywall to a garage wall and practice on them until you feel confident of the technique.

OPTIONS FOR THE BASE WALL AND TINTING PLASTER

BASE OPTIONS. If you are starting with a new wall, these are the two best options to ensure plaster adherence:

1. THE BACK SIDE of ordinary drywall can also be used as a plaster base.

2. BLUEBOARD, A POROUS gypsum sheet, is designed as a plaster base.

PLASTER OPTIONS. There are two ways to mix a tinted plaster.

The classic method is to mix 1 part plaster with approximately 2 parts water until the mixture resembles pudding. Then mix in artist's acrylic colors for the desired tint.

The second method is to add the color in the form of tinted acrylic latex paint. Use 1 quart of paint to 5 pounds of dry plaster. Mix only enough to eliminate the lumps.

3. TWO OPTIONS TO ACHIEVE the effect in the photograph on page 158:

Mix one part finishing plaster with two parts water and add Burnt Sienna artist's acrylic color until you reach the desired tint.

Or combine 1 quart of Burnt Sienna latex paint with 5 pounds of dry plaster. Mix only until lumps are gone.

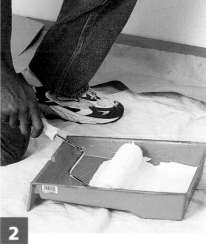

Preparing existing painted drywall. The plaster will need all the adhesion you can provide, and the thin layers of new plaster won't hide major flaws. Repair holes and wide cracks (pages 60–63). Kill off mildew or mold by washing it with a 3-to-1 solution of water and bleach. Scrub with a TSP solution. Rinse thoroughly. Using painter's masking tape, mask off the room.

If the paint has a semigloss or gloss finish, sand it lightly with a pad sander and 220-grit sandpaper. After wiping down the wall with a damp sponge or rag, prime the wall with an acrylic bonding agent.

1 **IT IS CRITICAL TO PREP** existing painted drywall. Repair major flaws and thoroughly scrub the walls with a TSP solution. Rinse with clean water.

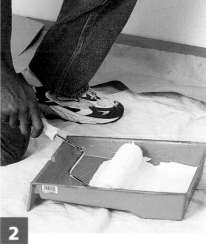

2 **TO ENSURE THE ADHESION** of the new plaster to the painted drywall, prime the wall with an acrylic bonding agent, available at paint centers.

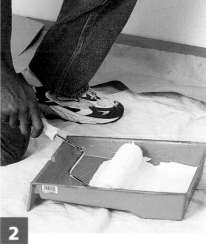

DECORATIVE PAINTING TECHNIQUES

159

SOUTHWESTERN TEXTURING (continued)

Applying the plaster finish. It is best to start on a small wall—a bathroom, an entrance, or a fireplace surround—because of the speed with which you have to work. The working time for a batch of plaster is about 45 minutes, and the entire wall must be completed in one operation. Otherwise the seams between batches will shrink and crack. Professional plasterers work in teams: one person to prepare the mix, and two or more to apply the plaster to the wall.

If you want to tackle a large room, perfect your technique on a small wall, then train and supervise several interested and capable friends.

A forgiving surface. Plaster doesn't dry like paint; it sets. Setting is a process of hydration—a chemical reaction wherein the water in the mix is absorbed. The plaster therefore "dries" from the inside out. That is why you can continue smoothing and burnishing its surface until it is completely set.

A plastic auto-body trowel is smoother and more flexible than a metal trowel and produces a tighter, shinier surface. Burnishing is polishing. The more you burnish, the smoother the surface will be.

Safety first. Because you're using a trowel rather than a roller with an extension, you'll do a lot of climbing up and down the stepladder. Lock the snapping bars into place and firmly position the ladder before you use it. Never stand on the top two steps. Wear shoes with slip-resistant soles.

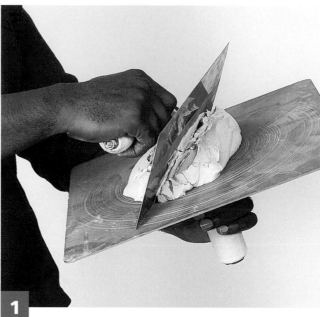

1 **LOAD THE MASON'S HAWK** with fresh plaster. Load the plasterer's trowel from the mason's hawk.

2 **APPLY THE FIRST ⅛-INCH COAT** of plaster to the wall using sweeping arcs. Get the plaster onto the wall quickly because it sets up in about 45 minutes.

3 **SMOOTH THIS FIRST COAT** of plaster with horizontal strokes of the trowel held nearly parallel to the plane of the wall.

4 **AFTER THE FIRST COAT IS DRY, APPLY A SECOND ⅛-INCH COAT** of plaster, again using sweeping arcs. Smooth this coat of plaster with vertical strokes.

CLOSE LOOK

avoid gouges

USE EVEN, STEADY PRESSURE to apply plaster to the wall. If there is too much pressure on one edge of the trowel, you may gouge the surface of the wall. Be especially careful to avoid such gouges in corners and tight spots.

QUICK TIP Gain depth in the finished wall by adding a coat of tinted glaze before you apply the final sealer.

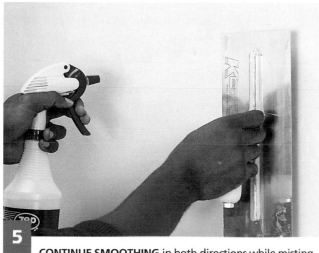

5 **CONTINUE SMOOTHING** in both directions while misting the surface with a spray bottle of water.

6 **WHEN THE PLASTER IS NEARLY DRY,** mist it and burnish it with a plastic auto-body trowel.

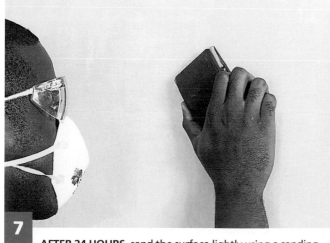

7 **AFTER 24 HOURS,** sand the surface lightly using a sanding block with 220-grit sandpaper and wipe up the dust with a damp cloth. Use a pole sander to make sanding the upper reaches of the wall easier.

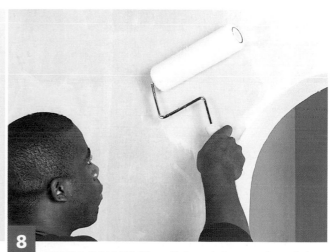

8 **APPLY A CLEAR-COAT** acrylic-based plaster sealer to help keep the plaster clean.

DECORATIVE PAINTING TECHNIQUES

STIPPLING

For a fine texture that adds depth and enhances your color selection, stipple paint over the base coat.

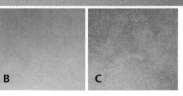

STUFF YOU'LL NEED

TOOLS: Utility knife, scrubbing sponge, bucket, rubber gloves, 4-foot stepladder, putty knife, sanding block, 9-inch roller cage with extension handle, dust mask, stippling brush, shaving brush, scissors, paint stirrer

MATERIALS: 12-inch baseboard masking, 2-inch painter's masking tape, drop cloth, TSP solution, crack filler or joint compound, primer, $3/8$-inch nap roller cover, 220-grit sandpaper, clean cotton cloths, glazing liquid, acrylic latex paint(s)

STIPPLING IS A SUBTRACTIVE PROCESS. It involves applying glaze over a base coat and then lifting some of the wet glaze off the wall with the tips of a dry stippling brush. It is similar to the technique of sponging off except it creates a much more finely textured surface. It is also more time-consuming because it requires "pouncing" or bouncing the brush over every square inch of the surface.

Stippling brushes with their tightly bunched and long, soft bristles can be expensive, but no other brush will give you as subtle a result. Edge stipplers have a narrow design that makes it easier to work in corners and along edges.

Stippling can also be an additive effect. A brush is dipped in the glaze mixture and applied to the wall by lightly slapping the bristles against the palm of your hand, spattering tiny drops of paint on the base coat.

PAINT CHIP COLORS: (below, left) **A)** Base coat: Willow River. Glaze: Green Gable. **B)** Base coat: Daffodil Hill. Glaze: Surrey Beige. **C)** Base coat: Bridal White. Glaze: Sea Cove.

Wall preparation. You obviously want people to admire the walls in your home—that is why you are applying a decorative paint technique. Holes, dents, cracks, and peeling paint can ruin the effect you work so hard to achieve.

Prepare the wall before you roll on even the base coat of paint. Repair surface mars. Kill off mildew and mold by washing with a 3-to-1 solution of water and bleach. Wash the walls with a TSP solution. Rinse thoroughly. Refer to pages 56–67 for details.

Apply primer even if there is an old coat of finish paint on the wall. Primers are specifically designed to stick to the wall and provide the ideal base for a new coat of paint. This is especially important when you are applying a decorative finish.

1 **AFTER CLEANING AND PREPPING THE WALL,** mask all adjacent surfaces with painter's masking tape. This special tape is less likely to lift paint than ordinary masking tape.

2 **APPLY THE PRIMER RECOMMENDED** by your paint center, then roll on a base coat of semigloss acrylic latex paint. Allow the base coat to dry for 24 hours before applying a decorative finish.

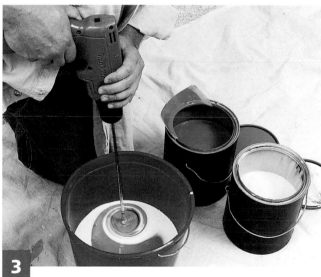

3 **MIX THE GLAZE** in a ratio of one part paint to four parts glaze as directed by the manufacturer.

GOOD IDEA

teamwork works best

Stippling is time-consuming. Have an assistant roll on the glaze just ahead of you to keep it from drying before you get to it. When you decide to switch jobs, do so at a natural break in the wall. That will help make the difference in your techniques less noticeable.

STIPPLING (continued)

Brush stippling. Stippling requires the right glaze conditions. If it is too thick and wet, the stipples will disappear as the glaze flows together. If the glaze is too thin and dry, the brush will have little effect. If you have trouble achieving the right glaze conditions, roll it on thickly, then brush it out with a fairly dry brush just before stippling. The brush will reduce the thickness, but leave the glaze wet.

If the base doesn't show through enough, just keep stippling. The brush removes more of the glaze with each pounce. Step back and view your progress periodically. Don't take too long a break or you may have trouble blending the wet glaze with the dry. Work one wall at a time so you don't see the differences in technique that are natural as you become more adept with the stippling brush.

4 **STARTING AT ONE END** of the wall, cut in the corner and the first several feet of the wall, ceiling, and baseboard joints with a 2-inch trim or sash brush.

5 **ROLL AN 18-INCH STRIP** from ceiling to floor using a 9-inch roller cover with ⅜-inch nap. Make sure you overlap the cut-in sections.

6 **AS SOON AS YOU HAVE ROLLED** the first 18-inch strip, have your assistant begin stippling: first the corner with a small brush and then the wide strip.

7 **CONTINUE CUTTING IN AND ROLLING** 18-inch strips while your assistant stipples. Don't get too far ahead or the glaze may dry before it is stippled.

the right tool for the job

AN EDGE STIPPLING BRUSH can be expensive, but it's a good investment because you'll get a better job in corners and along edges. If the surface you are stippling is small, however, you can make your own brush by trimming the bristles of an old-fashioned shaving brush to a flat tip.

OTHER STIPPLING APPLICATION OPTIONS

USE CHEESECLOTH. Because of its open weave, cheesecloth is an excellent, and less expensive, alternative to the stippling brush. Cut the cloth into 2-foot squares. Make a "bolster rag" by balling up one piece and wrapping it in a second piece. Pounce the bolster rag straight on and off the wall. Rewrap the bolster when it fills with glaze.

1. BOUNCE (POUNCE) THE BALLED-UP cheesecloth straight on and off the wall. If you accidentally smear the paint, quickly roll over the smear and pounce again.

2. TEXTURE DEPENDS ON CHEESECLOTH absorbing the glaze. Before it becomes saturated, re-ball the inner piece of cheesecloth and replace the outer one.

USE A HOT DOG ROLLER. A small foam roller, known as a hot dog roller because of its shape and size, produces a finish between the stipple-brush finish and solid color. The glaze is applied with one roller, then stippled, or partially removed, with a dry hot dog roller. When the stippling roller becomes saturated, dry it by rolling it over clean, lint-free cloth or paper towels.

3. ROLL THE DRY FOAM HOT DOG ROLLER in random directions. Keep an eye out for a change in the texture, indicating too much paint on the roller.

4. AS SOON AS THE STIPPLED TEXTURE begins to change, remove the paint from the hot dog roller by rolling over clean, dry cloths or paper towels.

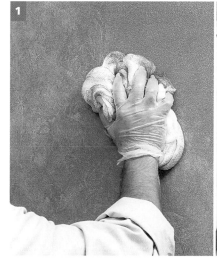

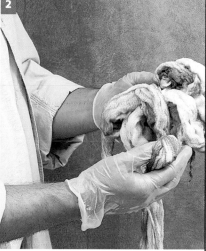

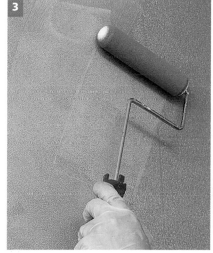

FRESCO
COLOR WASHING

Emulate the aura of old-world living by applying this technique.

FRESCO IS A CROSS BETWEEN Southwestern texturing and color washing. It consists of troweling an uneven skim coat of drywall joint compound onto drywall and then color-washing the surface. The resulting wall has a rustic, old-world look, reminiscent of the walls in ancient homes in France. If done without care or proper wall prep, however, the wall can look like an attempt to hide the drywall joints without taping and sanding.

The technique requires a thin (⅛ inch) skim coat of joint compound. While this application will fill small holes and dents, you should repair gouges and wide cracks (see pages 56–63). Clean the walls, then plaster, paint, glaze, and blend for a beautiful finish with depth and texture.

PAINT CHIP COLORS: (below, left) **A)** Base coat: Ivory Candle. Glaze: Sage Leaf mixed with White. **B)** Base coat: White Whisper. Glaze: Scenic Rose. **C)** Base coat: Ultra Pure White. Glaze: Sweet Butter.

STUFF YOU'LL NEED

TOOLS: Utility knife, scrubbing sponge, bucket, rubber gloves, 4-foot stepladder, sanding block, dust mask, 9-inch roller cage with extension handle, plaster trowel, two 3-inch brushes, 4-inch brush

MATERIALS: 12-inch baseboard masking, 2-inch painter's masking tape, drop cloth, TSP solution, drywall joint compound, primer, ¾-inch nap roller cover, 220-grit sandpaper, clean cotton cloths, acrylic latex paints

A

B   C

Preparing the base. Drywall joint compound will cover minor blemishes, such as nail holes, dings, and dents, but it still needs to adhere to the wall. Neither paint nor joint compound will stick well to a dusty or greasy wall, so you need to rid the wall of dirt and grease by scrubbing with a TSP solution and then rinsing thoroughly.

If the wall has an existing coat of paint, sand it lightly with 220-grit sandpaper to increase the adhesion.

If the wall is unpainted drywall, tape the joints to prevent cracking. Sand, remove all dust, and then prime the entire wall with PVA primer (see page 69), which is formulated to seal the dry paper face.

WORK SMARTER

the voice of experience

SOME TIPS for better results:

1. Drywall compound is formulated to dry quickly. To stretch its drying time, humidify the space you are working in or apply the compound on a cool, humid day.

2. Keep the layer of joint compound thin—⅛ inch maximum—because a thicker layer will develop hairline cracks.

3. As you trowel on the compound, never return any unused portion to the original container, and immediately discard any compound that contains hardened material. Lumps in the compound will leave tracks as they are dragged across the surface. You will spend valuable time (and endure frustration) picking out the lumps. The cost of additional compound is minimal in comparison.

1

BOTH SKIM COATING AND COLOR WASHING are messy projects, so after prepping the wall, lay a drop cloth and overlap it with 12-inch baseboard masking.

GOOD IDEA

minimize dust

Sanding drywall compound produces an extremely fine dust, which will diffuse through your home. To minimize dust flow, hang damp sheets in doorways and lightly mist the drywall with a spray bottle. Then don a paper mask and, using wet-or-dry sandpaper, sand the walls to remove ridges.

2

STARTING AT AN UPPER CORNER, apply a ⅛-inch layer of joint compound. If you find the large plaster trowel unwieldy, you can use a 6- or 12-inch putty knife.

3

CONTINUE APPLYING COMPOUND from top to bottom, sweeping the trowel randomly to create raised ridges. The goal is not a smooth surface.

FRESCO COLOR WASHING (continued)

The application. Fresco color washing is a perfect treatment for walls in sound but rough shape. The ⅛-inch thickness of joint compound automatically fills minor holes, dents, and rough spots.

Since the ⅛-inch maximum coating won't crack, you don't have to finish the entire job in one session, as you do with plaster in Southwestern texturing. Finishing at a natural break, such as a corner or a door molding, however, will make seams less noticeable.

The entire process works best when there are two, or even three, people wielding brushes. Two people apply a glaze, and the third person blends the glazes together.

With two workers, take turns blending the glazes. Switch positions at a natural break, such as a corner, so the difference in technique won't be so obvious.

If you are working alone, reduce the size of the sections by half (to about 2×3 feet) so the glaze remains wet until you can get it blended.

4   **ALLOW THE COMPOUND TO DRY,** indicated by a lack of gray spots. Sand lightly with a sanding block and 220-grit sandpaper to remove sharp ridges and bumps.

5   **APPLY PVA PRIMER** (formulated for drywall) using a 9-inch roller cover with a ¾-inch nap. Allow the primer to dry for at least 24 hours.

6   **APPLY AN EGGSHELL-FINISH** base coat for the color wash, using the roller with another ¾-inch nap cover. Allow the base coat to dry for two days.

7   **MIX YOUR FIRST GLAZE** using a ratio of one part paint to four parts glaze as directed by the manufacturer. To make the second glaze, pour one-third of the first glaze into another container. Add an equal amount of white paint and mix.

8 **STARTING AT AN UPPER CORNER,** apply the first glaze in random strokes with a 3-inch brush, covering about one-third of a 3×4-foot area.

9 **WITH A SECOND 3-INCH BRUSH,** apply the second glaze, covering another one-third of the same 3×4-foot area. Don't paint over the first glaze.

10 **WHILE BOTH GLAZES ARE STILL WET,** use a 4-inch brush to blend the two glazes with random strokes. Work the glaze until you achieve the desired effect.

11 **REPEAT STEPS 8 TO 10** for the next 3×4-foot section, blending the two areas together. It is easier to keep wet edges if two people work together.

DECORATIVE PAINT FILE

how to get the look

The fresco color-washing technique was used on these entry walls. Note that the texture complements adjacent tile and wood surfaces and conceals minor surface flaws.

AGING

Add a patina of instant age to brand-new wallpaper or paint using this smoke-stain technique.

STUFF YOU'LL NEED

TOOLS: Utility knife, scrubbing sponge, bucket, rubber gloves, 4-foot stepladder, hot dog roller, roller tray, stirring stick

MATERIALS: 12-inch baseboard masking, 2-inch painter's masking tape, drop cloth, TSP solution, hot dog roller covers, base coat latex paint (if not wallpapered), clear sealer (if wallpapered), glazing liquid, raw umber tint or tube of acrylic artist's paint

WALLPAPER TENDS TO PICK UP airborne smoke particles and droplets of cooking oil, gradually darkening over time. In fact, yellow-brown wallpaper is automatically assumed to be old.

If "old" is the look you want to create, you can add a patina of smoke stain in an afternoon. You just add raw umber tint (available at most paint centers) or raw umber watercolor paint (available at art supply stores) to latex glaze (the translucent body of latex paint without any color) and apply it to the wallpaper.

The trick is not to overdo the effect. At some point the wallpaper will look so old you may want to replace it. Practice with sample boards, allowing them to fully dry before passing judgment. Even then, err on the light side. Remember: You can always darken the wall further with another application, but you can't lighten it by removing glaze that is already down. Some aging glazes can be purchased premixed at the store. Check with your local paint center to see if they are available.

Aging technique on painted wall

Repair first. If the wallpaper isn't in good shape to begin with, what you will end up with is not just an antique patina, but a wall that looks like it should be repapered. In that case, strip the paper and start over. (see "Removing Wallpaper" on pages 48–50.)

Don't confuse glazing liquid, which is colorless, with a latex-tint base, which contains at least white pigment. The translucent glazing liquid will allow the wallpaper pattern to show through undiminished. If you use a latex-tint base, it will cover the pattern like white paint. Make sure your paint salesperson understands the effect you are trying to achieve. And buy translucent glazing liquid, not latex-tint base.

1   **IF THE WALL IS WALLPAPERED,** apply a clear sealer. The sealer will not discolor the paper but will prevent the stain from soaking into the paper unevenly.

2   **MAKE A SMOKE-STAIN GLAZE** by adding raw umber tint or artist's acrylic paint to translucent latex glaze. Experiment with test panels to gauge the amount of color to add.

3   **APPLY THE GLAZE WITH A ROLLER** as you would any paint. If the effect isn't strong enough after the first coat dries, apply a second coat of glaze.

AGING PAINTED WALLS

IF THE WALL IS NOT wallpapered, you can still add instant age with a smoke-stain glaze.

Repair mars, holes, and dents (see pages 56–63). Wash the walls with a TSP solution and rinse thoroughly. Mask the room. Prime the walls; allow primer to dry for 24 hours. Apply a base coat and allow it to dry. Then glaze. The lighter the base coat, the more apparent the smoke-stain effect.

CRACKLE

It can take decades for oil paint to crack; with this technique, the aging process will take hours, not years.

STUFF YOU'LL NEED

TOOLS: Rubber gloves, pad sander, dust mask, two 2-inch foam brushes, 2-inch nylon brush

MATERIALS: Piece of painted or unfinished furniture, 80-, 110-, and 220-grit sandpaper, white-pigmented shellac sealer/primer, flat acrylic latex base coat, eggshell acrylic latex top coat, crackle medium (all from same manufacturer), clear water-based polyurethane sealer

AS OIL-BASED PAINTS AGE, they turn brittle. When an underlying wood base shrinks and swells with moisture, the paint cracks, much like dried mud in a puddle. The pattern that emerges is called crackling, and nothing makes a piece of furniture look older.

You can "age" an old bureau or table in a few hours by painting crackle medium over a base coat, letting it dry, and then applying a top coat. The crackle medium will cause the top coat to crack, exposing the base coat below. The darker the base coat, the more obvious the crackling.

The effect is somewhat unpredictable, and you get but one chance unless you are willing to strip the paint and start over. It is safest to buy the same brand of crackle medium and top coat because they have been formulated to work together.

Start small. It may be tempting to crackle a large piece of furniture, but with this technique you need to get it right the first time. So start with a small piece, such as a picture frame. For the best results, allow each coat to dry thoroughly before applying the next layer. Never try to rebrush the top coat; it will lift the paint and you'll have to start over. **PAINT CHIP COLORS: Picture frame.** Base coat: Country Trail. Top coat: Magma. **Dresser.** Base coat: Country Trail. Top coat: Lawn Chair.

Crackle technique on frame

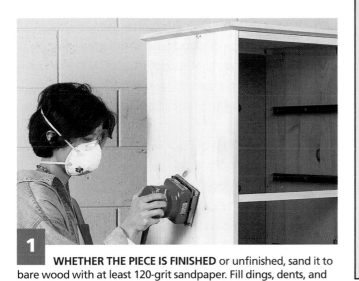

1 WHETHER THE PIECE IS FINISHED or unfinished, sand it to bare wood with at least 120-grit sandpaper. Fill dings, dents, and holes with wood filler.

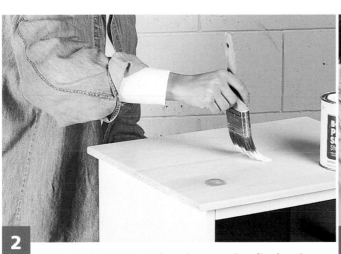

2 SPOT PRIME KNOTS, pitch pockets, or other discoloration. Then prime the entire surface with white-pigmented shellac.

3 APPLY THE BASE COAT. If the first coat is rough, sand after 24 hours with 220-grit sandpaper and apply a second base coat.

DECORATIVE PAINTING TECHNIQUES

4 APPLY THE CRACKLE MEDIUM with a brush and let it dry as long as recommended by the manufacturer.

5 APPLY A FLAT or eggshell top coat with a foam brush. Restrain yourself! If you go back and rebrush, the paint will lift and you will have to start over.

6 TO TOUGHEN the crackled surface, wait about a month and apply a coat of clear water-based polyurethane or a product recommended by the crackle manufacturer.

ANTIQUING

Add decades to the life of a piece of furniture in hours by antiquing the finish.

STUFF YOU'LL NEED

TOOLS: Rubber gloves, pad sander, dust mask, two 2-inch foam brushes, 2-inch nylon brush, several keys attached to a large key ring

MATERIALS: Piece of painted or unfinished furniture, 80-, 110-, and 220-grit sandpaper, white-pigmented shellac sealer/primer, flat acrylic latex base coat, eggshell acrylic latex top coat, clear water-based polyurethane sealer

CLOSER LOOK

distressing news

DISTRESSING IMITATES the effects of real-life wear and tear. Tabletops are scuffed and scratched by knives, silverware, plates, dishes, and pans; table and chair legs are bumped together, causing scratches; paint on chair seats and backs is worn away with use. Sand sparingly to imitate wear; sand through paint to the wood in spots that typically receive the heaviest wear, such as edges, corners, and knob and handle areas.

IN THE 19TH CENTURY, most, if not all, furniture sported a coat of bright paint to bring color into the home. When its age began to show, the piece would be repainted—often in another color. Paint was the major redecorating tool of the time, just as it is today. Continued use caused the original color to wear through in exposed places, and that's what we simulate when we "antique" a piece of furniture. It's easy to do: Apply two (or three) coats of paint, distress, and sand the piece to simulate everyday wear and tear. Choose your color scheme, then sand, prime, and apply the base color following the instructions on page 171. Then you're ready to begin antiquing. Dings and chips are common on the surfaces of old furniture, so begin by distressing.

1 **DISTRESS THE SURFACE.** Put a combination of old and new keys on a large key ring. The variations will help to vary the texture. Holding the keys by the ring, randomly bounce them against the surface to simulate wear. Make a few scratches with a coin or a nail; scrape off some paint by dragging the edge of a knife across a couple of spots. Once the piece is properly distressed, resand to simulate more wear.

2 **APPLY, THEN DISTRESS, THE TOP COAT.** The color of the top coat contrasts with the base coat. Brush on the top coat, let it dry, and then distress this coat, using the techniques used previously. In occasional spots that would have received a lot of wear, sand through to the first coat, and then sand through part of the first coat to reveal the wood. Elsewhere, sand through the paint just enough to reveal the first coat. Repeat, if desired, with a third color and distress it, also.

GOOD IDEA

go easy when you distress wooden furniture

Working slowly allows you to see and re-create the effects of time and hard use. You can always intensify or add a dent or a scrape. No matter how much fun it may seem at the time of distressing, it takes time and effort to sand out the results of aggressive thumping and banging.

SPONGE PAINTING, a technique for applying color over a base coat, achieves a multitone finish. A sponge-painted surface has a subtle and natural character that is more interesting than a plain-painted surface. It's not used to imitate a particular effect but suggests fabric, stone, leaves, or a cloud-filled patch of sky. Commonly used on walls, sponging also works well on furniture—especially to differentiate one surface from another.

Though you can sponge on a finish with plain paint, it works better when a glazing liquid is mixed with the paint. The glazing liquid has more body than paint and gives the sponged surface more depth and texture. It also makes the mixture workable for a longer period of time than plain paint. Follow the manufacturer's instructions for mixing the glazing liquid and paint.

A natural sea sponge works best to apply the glaze mix, although a synthetic sponge also can be used. Choose one that fits comfortably in your hand.

Sponging works as well on furniture as it does on walls, adding depth and beauty to ready-to-finish pieces.

STUFF YOU'LL NEED

TOOLS: Plastic bucket, rubber gloves, safety goggles or glasses, sea sponge, rollers or brushes

MATERIALS: Piece of painted or unfinished furniture, 80-, 110-, and 220-grit sandpaper, white-pigmented shellac sealer/primer, flat acrylic latex base coat, eggshell acrylic latex glaze coat, clear water-based polyurethane sealer, paper plate, paper towels

CLOSER LOOK

natural vs. synthetic sponges

BECAUSE THEY'RE NOT MAN MADE, each sea sponge is one of a kind. The holes vary in size and shape and the texture is irregular. That irregularity is what makes sea sponges more effective for faux finishing techniques. They hold more paint and reduce repetitive patterns on the surface you're painting.

1 MIX THE PAINT AND GLAZE. Glaze may be white or translucent—mix 4 parts glaze to 1 part paint to achieve the color you want. To keep the color constant, mix enough to do the entire job. The directions on the label will give you an idea of how much you need for a specific area. Once you mix the glaze, pour into a flat container.

2 SPONGE ON THE GLAZE. Dampen a sponge in water to help it absorb the glaze. Dip the sponge in the glaze and paint mixture, and then dab it on a paper plate or paper towel to remove the excess. If the paint drips when you apply it, dab more onto the plate. Apply the paint with a light touch. Work in random patterns or in rows, and rotate the sponge so that the pattern constantly changes. Cover a 4×4-foot section, and do the edges last so that they're wet and blend easily into the next section.

3 ADD A SECOND COLOR. If you apply a second color, wait at least 48 hours for the first coat of glaze to dry thoroughly. After you finish each section, stand back to look at your work. If you see lines or patterns, blot on a little more glaze to break them up. Apply the next section, working from the wet edge. Sponge on the second color the same as you applied the first.

6

CLEANING UP

IN THIS SECTION: the final step

YOU'RE NOT FINISHED PAINTING until you clean up! This chapter offers hints to make even cleanup easier. It starts during painting: Wipe up spatters and spills as you go. When you're finished, take proper care of brushes and rollers for your next painting project.

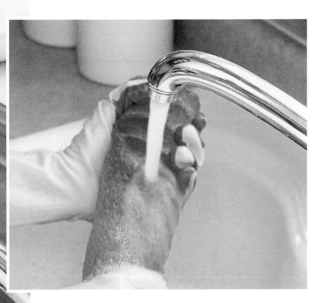

CLEANUP MAY NOT BE exciting, but it's just as important as any other part of the job. Take good care of your tools and they'll take good care of you!

CLEANING BRUSHES

A good brush deserves the care to preserve it. Carefully cleaned, a high-quality brush can last for years.

LATEX PAINT

MANY PROFESSIONAL painters have favorite brushes they have used for years. With proper care, a high-quality brush will see you through multiple paint projects.

Taking care of a brush means never letting paint dry on the bristles, cleaning it completely when a job is finished, and storing it properly with the bristles in a protective sleeve.

If you have to remove dried paint from a brush, use brush cleaner, which is formulated to remove paint without destroying the brush. Stay away from paint removers; they are too hard on the bristles.

1 **BRUSH OUT** as much of the paint as you can on a newspaper or other disposable surface.

2 **HOLD THE BRUSH** under warm running water until the water runs clear.

3 **IF HARDENED PAINT** remains against the ferrule, use a wire paint comb to dislodge it.

4 **WASH THE BRUSH** with warm dish detergent or TSP solution, working it up into the ferrule.

UP TO CODE

safe cleaning

MANY STATES HAVE BANNED cleaning brushes in a sink. If yours is one of them, use this three-can process:

- Half fill each of three cans with water (latex paints) or paint thinner (oil-based paints).
- Soak the brush in the first can, moving it up, down, and sideways to remove most of the paint.
- Repeat the process in can #2, and then again in can #3.
- Dry the brush by slapping the ferrule on the heel of your hand and pressing the bristles between paper towels.

Allow the solids to settle. Pour thinner into clean cans for reuse. After the solids have dried, trash them.

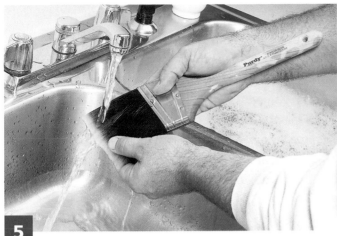

5 **RINSE AGAIN** under clear warm water until all traces of paint have been removed.

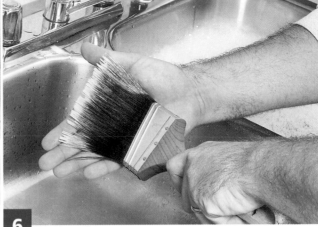

6 **SLAP THE BRISTLES** against your palm several times to remove excess water.

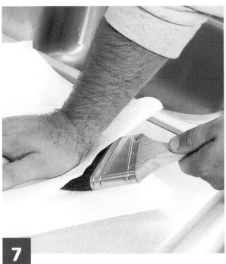

7 **BLOT THE BRISTLES** between 3 to 4 sheets of paper towel, applying pressure with the heel of your hand.

8 **REPLACE THE BRUSH** in its original cardboard holder. Hang it vertically.

GOOD IDEA

custom brush covers

If the original cardboard brush holder is lost, you can make a replacement cover from a shirt cardboard. Fold the cardboard tightly around the ferrule, mark it, then remove and staple together.

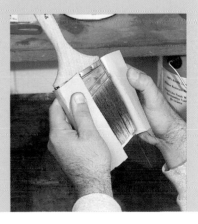

TRIP SAVER

substitute

IF YOU DON'T HAVE a wire paint comb, use a pet comb or an ordinary plastic pocket comb. When it comes to brush care, any attempt at cleaning is better than none.

CLEANING UP

OIL-BASED PAINT

CLEANING OIL-BASED PAINT from brushes involves the same steps as latex paint, using paint thinner instead of water, except you can't pour thinner down the drain. (You may not be able to pour paintbrush water down the drain either—see "Up to Code" on page 178.)

Because paint thinner must be captured, use the three-can process demonstrated below. If the paint has already hardened at all, substitute brush cleaner— a more aggressive solvent—for paint thinner in the first can.

When you have finished cleaning brushes, let the cans of thinner settle. After a few days you can pour off the clear thinner for reuse. Allow the solids to dry in the cans, then dispose of them as recommended by your local waste management authority.

Wear gloves when you work with paint thinner.

1 **LABEL THREE CLEAN** 1-pound coffee cans 1, 2, and 3 with a permanent marker. Fill each can half full with paint thinner.

2 **BRUSH OUT AS MUCH** of the paint as you can on a newspaper or other disposable surface.

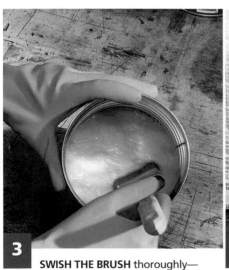

3 **SWISH THE BRUSH** thoroughly— sideways and up and down—in can 1.

4 **BRUSH OUT** as much of the thinner as you can on the newspaper.

5 **REPEAT THE PROCESS** in steps 3 and 4 with cans 2 and 3.

6 **IF ANY HARDENED PAINT** remains lodged against the ferrule, use a wire comb to dislodge it.

7 **WASH THE BRISTLES** with a warm detergent or TSP solution, forcing the liquid up into the ferrule.

8 **RINSE THE DETERGENT** solution from the bristles with warm running water.

9 **REMOVE MOST** of the water by slapping the ferrule and letting the bristles whip.

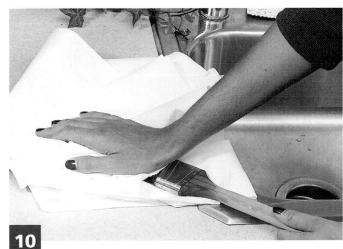

10 **PLACE THE BRISTLES** between 3 to 4 layers of paper towel and blot with the heel of your hand.

11 **HANG THE BRUSH** by its handle in the original paper cover or one you make (see page 179).

CLEANING ROLLER COVERS

Follow these steps to remove latex paint from a roller cover. Clean the cage even if you don't save the cover.

ROLLER COVERS ARE LESS expensive than high-quality brushes, don't last as long, and are more difficult to clean. Consequently, the pros often consider them disposable. However, you still may want to clean a high-quality roller cover.

All of the warnings about disposing of water-thinned latex and solvents down a drain apply to the cleaning of rollers as well. Read about the disposal of waste water on page 178 and paint thinner on page 180.

Clean the cage, too. Whether you choose to clean the cover or not, don't forget to clean the roller cage. Removing even hardened paint from the metal cage is relatively simple. Use a wire brush if the paint has hardened.

These photographs show how to clean latex paint from a roller cover. Even the professionals don't try to salvage covers used for oil-based paints.

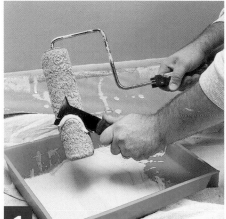

1 **REMOVE AS MUCH** excess paint as possible by scraping the roller with a handy 5-in-1 tool.

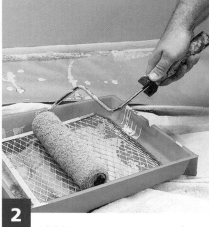

2 **LOOSEN THE ROLLER FIBERS** by rolling on a paint tray grid.

3 **USING RUBBER GLOVES,** pull the roller cover off the wire cage.

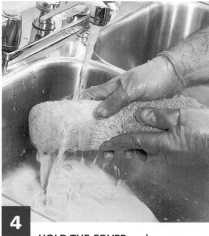

4 **HOLD THE COVER** under warm running water until the water runs nearly clear.

 TOOL TIP

too tired to clean?

YOU CAN KEEP A WET ROLLER overnight, either to use the next day, or to delay cleaning.

Put the roller cover in a self-locking, plastic bag and store it in the refrigerator. Or immerse the roller cover in water.

5 WASH THE COVER in warm water with dish detergent. Work the solution into the fibers.

6 RINSE THE DETERGENT solution out of the cover until the water runs totally clear.

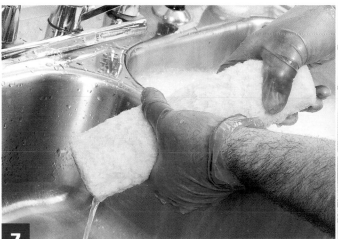

7 SQUEEZE OUT THE EXCESS water by sliding your circled forefinger and thumb down the roller. A roller and brush spinner will get excess water out quickly. Ask for one at your paint center.

8 DRY AND STORE the wet roller cover by hanging or standing it on end.

CLEANING YOURSELF

1. WASH YOUR SKIN in warm soapy water. Scrub resistant spots with a plastic scrub pad.

2. RUB HARDENED LATEX paint on clothing with a commercial cleanup product designed to remove hardened paint.

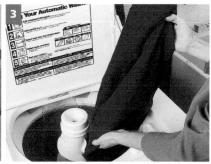

3. TO REMOVE the cleaner and paint residue, run the fabric through a normal wash cycle.

CLEANING UP

183

CLEANING SPILLS AND SPATTERS

Dried paint can be tough to remove. You'll save time if you make a habit of cleaning up as you go.

SPILLS AND SPATTERS are inevitable when you paint. Even professionals dribble and drip occasionally. But the difference between the pros and most of the rest of us is that they clean up as they go.

On a nonporous surface, any spill needs to be wiped up immediately with a clean cloth while the paint is still liquid. You have a little more time if you're using latex paint. Spray the splatter with clean water. Then wipe up the spill before you reload the brush.

Remove paint from fabric while it's still wet. The key is to dilute the paint with water, then wash it in a TSP solution.

You may not notice the paint on fabric until it has hardened. With latex paint, rub the fabric with a commercial paint cleaner. With oil-based paint, use brush cleaner. In both cases, finish by washing the fabric in a TSP solution.

KEEP A SPRAY BOTTLE of water handy when painting with latex. Spray drips and spatters and wipe immediately with a clean, soft cloth.

IF THE PAINT SPOTS have hardened too much to wet and wipe, scrub them with a wet plastic scrub pad, then wipe up.

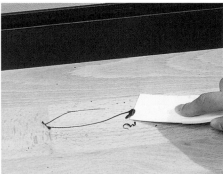

IF A SCRUB PAD doesn't work, pry the spots off carefully with a plastic or metal putty knife.

FOR OIL-BASED SPILLS, try wiping up drips with a dry cotton rag. If necessary, dampen the rag with a small amount of paint thinner or denatured alcohol.

STORAGE AND DISPOSAL

Save leftover paint for touch-ups and repairs. Stored properly, it can last as long as a coat of paint.

STORING PAINT

LATEX PAINT WILL STORE indefinitely, provided two conditions are met:

1. It doesn't freeze.
2. It is sealed in an airtight container.

The first condition is met by storage in a warm, dry location. The second requires either transferring the remainder to a new container or cleaning the rim of all hardened paint, which might interfere with the seal.

Even in an airtight container, the top layer of paint can dry, forming a "skin." It helps to store latex paint cans upside down. This keeps skinning to an absolute minimum. When you turn the can over to open it, the hardened skin will sink to the bottom of the can.

1 **IF THERE IS LESS** than one quart of paint left, transfer it to a clean, empty quart can.

2 **IF YOU ARE KEEPING** the original can, wipe up paint inside the rim with a small screwdriver wrapped in cloth.

3 **TAP THE LID DOWN** evenly with a block of wood and a hammer.

4 **PAINT A DAB** of the leftover paint on the lid with a cotton swab.

5 **WRITE THE PAINT** information on the lid with a permanent black marker.

DISPOSING OF PAINT AND SOLVENTS

LIQUID PAINTS and solvents can't be tossed out with the household trash—it's against the law. You must let them evaporate and solidify and then dispose of them in a manner recommended by your local waste management authority. Find a secure place to leave open cans (not in the house or another enclosed space) and leave the lids off until the contents are solidified.

To speed up the evaporation process, especially if you have a significant amount of liquid, add sawdust, vermiculite, or cat litter to the cans.

TO DISPOSE of old latex paint, mix it with sawdust or vermiculite, let it solidify, then take it to the dump.

PLACE SOLVENT RAGS in a can, fill with water, seal the can, and call your waste management authority for proper disposal.

CLEANING UP

185

INDEX

Page numbers in italics denote pages with photographs of decorative painting techniques

INDEX

ACKNOWLEDGEMENTS AND RESOURCES

Special thanks to the following organizations and corporations whose products and advice were instrumental in creating this book.

Additional Photography:
Doug Hetherington Photography
(515) 243-6329

The Glidden Company
1-800-GLIDDEN (454-3336)
www.glidden.com

**The Rohm and Haas Paint
Quality Institute**
John Stauffer
www.paintquality.com

**Delta Ceramcoat—Delta
Technical Coatings, Inc.**
(800) 423-4135
www.deltacrafts.com

Valspar Specialty Division
(800) 845-9061
www.valspar.com

Behr Process Corporation
3400 W. Segerstrom Ave.
Santa Ana, CA 92704
(714) 545-7101
Fax: (714) 545-1002
www.behrpaint.com

**Stencil Décor Paint by Plaid
Plaid Enterprises, Inc.**
(800) 842-4197
www.plaidonline.com

COLOR PALETTES

Sponging On – Page 108
Color Set A: Behr Paint
Base coat:
Moroccan Leather   TH-82
Glaze:
Opera House   TH-61

Color Set B: Behr Paint
Base coat:
Chocolate Mousse   TH-88
Glaze:
Nantucket Shingle   TH-46

Color Set C: Glidden paint
Base coat:
Lodestar   70gg 83/090
Glaze:
Springvale   10gg 63/194

Sponging Off – Page 112
Color Set A: Behr paint
Base coat:
Buttercream   CH-1
Glaze:
Yellow Ware   CH-5

Color Set B: Glidden paint
Base coat:
Green Gables   90gy 48/091
Glaze:
Gateway   10gy 17/127

Color Set C: Behr paint
Base coat:
Meyer Lemon   FF 23-1
Glaze:
Zesty Orange   FF 23-1

Ragging Off – Page 116
Color Set A: Glidden paint
Base coat:
Brass Rail   30yy 44/509
Glaze:
Starlet   45yy 83/187

Color Set B: Behr paint
Base coat:
Celestial Plume 3A34-3
Glaze:
Reverie   3A34-5

Color Set C: Behr paint
Base coat:
Rain Cloud   CH-49
Glaze:
Country Trail   CH-37

Ragging On – Page 120
Color Set A: Behr paint
Base coat:
Pagent Pink   IA26-4
Glaze:
Pink Icicle   4C13-2

Color Set B: Behr paint
Base coat:
Ivory Palm   4C3-2
Glaze:
Fernette   2A57-3

Color Set C: Glidden paint
Base coat:
Monte Carlo Blue 30bg 16/204
Glaze:
Jamaican Blue   30bg 50/156

Color Washing – Page 124
Color Set A: Behr paint
Base coat:
Chinese Export TH-56
Glaze:
Kayak   BHG-55

Color Set B: Behr paint
Base coat:
Young Gazelle   3A16-3
Glaze:
Windsor Castle 3A11-4

Color Set C: Glidden paint
Base coat:
Redware   104r 15/248
Glaze:
Snowfield   00nn 72/000

Faux Leather – Page 128
Color Set A: Behr paint
Base coat:
Gondola   3B11-6
Glaze:
Windsor Castle 3A11-4

Color Set B: Glidden paint
Base coat:
Bridal Gown   10yr 83/010
Glaze:
Glorius Plum   10rr 16/156
Suave Mauve   10rr 53/087

Color Set C: Behr paint
Base coat:
Skipping Rocks BHG-18

Glaze:
Snow Day   BHG-27
Sneakers   BHG-9

Double Rolling – Page 132
Color Set A: Behr paint
Base coat:
Wheatfield   3A10-4
Glaze:
Crepe De Chine 4C5-2

Color Set B: Glidden paint
Base coat:
Snow Bell   10bb 73/045
Glaze:
Paris Night   10bb 42/159

Color Set C: Behr paint
Base coat:
Frosted Pane   BHG-46
Glaze:
Green Glade   TH-67

Stenciling
Borders – Page 136
Color Set A: Glidden paint
Base coat:
Starlet   45yy 83/187
Stencil: custom made
Stencil Décor Paint by Plaid:
Wild Ivy   #26126
Dark Sapphire   #26115
Kiwi Green   #26147
Berry Red   #26111

Color Set B: Glidden paint
Base coat:
Oceantide   66bg 68/157
Stencil: custom made
Delta Ceramcoat Acrylic Paint:
Phthalo Green   #02501
Black   #02506
Barn Red   #26111
Antique Gold   #02002
Light Ivory   #02401
Sunbright Yellow   #02064

Color Set C: Behr paint
Base coat:
Buttercream Frosting   CH-1
Stencil: custom made
Delta Ceramcoat Acrylic Paint:
Phthalo Green   #02501
Ultra Blue   #02038
Liberty Blue   #02416
Black   #02506

Barn Red   #26111
Antique Gold   #02002
Sunbright Yellow   #02064
Dusty Mauve   #02405

Color Set D and E: Glidden paint
Base coat:
Brass Rail   30yy 44/509
Stencil: custom made
Delta Ceramcoat Acrylic Paint:
Phthalo Green   #02501
Bright Red   #02503
Light Ivory   #02401
Barn Red   #02490
Antique Gold   #02002

Dragging – Page 140
  Color Set A: Behr paint
  Base coat:
  Churned Butter CH-2
  Glaze:
  Skinned Knee   BHG-39

  Color Set B: Glidden paint
  Base coat:
  Whispering Wind   70gg 74/105
  Glaze:
  Floridian   30bg 50/237

  Color Set C: Behr paint
  Base coat:
  Ballerina   1B27-2
  Glaze:
  Pageant Pink   1A26-4

Combing – Page 144
  Color Set A: Behr paint
  Base coat:
  Knoll Green   3B1-6
  Glaze:
  Polynesia   3A3-5

  Color Set B: Behr paint
  Base coat:
  Mud Puddle   BHG-21
  Glaze:
  Pottery   BHG-82

  Color Set C: Glidden paint
  Base coat:
  Dapper Tan   10yy 55/163
  Glaze:
  Blue Angels   30bb 22/232

Spattering Colors – Page 152
  Color Set A: Glidden paint
  Base coat:
  Hawaiian Waters   30bg 28/183
  Spatters:
  Silver Springs   70gg 48/133
  Blue Bow   70bg 72/069

Blackfeet   30gg 09/025
Thin with water as necessary to make spattering easier.

  Color Set B: Glidden paint
  Base coat:
  Barrister White   30yy 80/088
  Spatters:
  Basket Tree   20yy 31/205
  Side Saddle   90yr 17/245
  Stone Grey   30yy 31/024

  Color Set C: Behr paint
  Base coat:
  Ultra Pure White   4C8-2
  Spatters:
  Epic Blue   5C13-3
  Beyond Red   4C10-3
  Yellow Cluster   4C1-3
  Green Court   5C4-3

Faux Marbling – Page 156
  Color Set: Behr paint
  Base coat:
  Ink Black   5C21-1
  Glaze:
  Woodsman Green   3B57-6
  Veining:
  White   4C8-2
  Stipple base:
  Fox Hollow   3A59-5
  Stipple glaze:
  Smoky Emerald   3A59-3

Southwestern Texturing – Page 158
  Color Set: Valspar Specialty Division
  Colored tint:
  Burnt Sienna   #372
  Recipe:
      1 part finishing plaster
      2 parts water
      Add paint until desired tint
      is acquired
      OR
      1 quart paint
      5 pounds dry plaster

Stippling – Page 162
  Color Set A: Behr paint
  Base coat:
  Willow River   3A1-4
  Glaze:
  Green Gable   2B56-6

  Color Set B: Glidden paint
  Base coat:
  Daffodil Hill   60yy 75/454
  Glaze:
  Surrey Beige   30yy 36/185

  Color Set C: Behr paint
  Base coat:
  Bridal White   BHG-26
  Glaze:
  Sea Cove   BHG-53

Fresco Color Washing – Page 166
  Color Set A: Behr paint
  Base coat:
  Ivory Candle   4C6-2
  Glaze:
  Sage Leaf   CH-63
  Mix Sage Leaf and white for additional color

  Color Set B: Glidden paint
  Base coat:
  White Whisper   44yy 84/042
  Glaze:
  Scenic Rose   30yr 16/286

  Color Set C: Behr paint
  Base coat:
  Ultra Pure White   4C8-2
  Glaze:
  Sweet Butter   1A1-4

Aging – Page 170
  Wallpaper:
  Add Raw Umber Acrylic: tint to translucent glaze. Quantity will be based on how aged you want the wall to look.

  Painted wall: Glidden paint
  Brass Rail   30yy 44/509

Crackle – Page 172
  Picture Frame: Behr paint
  Base coat:
  Country Trail   CH-37
  Crackle medium:
  Magma   3B42-6

  Dresser: Behr paint
  Base coat:
  Country Trail   CH-37
  Crackle medium:
  Lawn Chair   BHG-56

Antiquing – Page 174
  Color Set: Behr paint
  Base coat:
  Sashay Red   4C9-3
  Top coat:
  Night Sea   2B45-6

Sponging – Page 175
  Color Set: Behr paint
  Base coat:
  Vermouth   3B1-1
  Top coat:
  Pine Song   2B60-6

Toolbox essentials: nuts-and-bolts books for do-it-yourself success.

Save money, get great results, and take the guesswork out of home improvement projects with a growing library of step-by-step books from the experts at The Home Depot®

Packed with lots of projects and practical tips, these books help you design, remodel, decorate, and repair your home or garden. Easy-to-follow, step-by-step instructions and colorful photographs ensure success. Projects even estimate time, skills, materials needed, and tools required.

Look for the books that help you say "I can do that!" at The Home Depot®, www.meredithbooks.com, or wherever quality books are sold.

PAINT
ESTIMATOR

How Much Paint Will You Need ?

WALLS

1 **CALCULATE THE WALL AREA:**

Multiply the length of each wall by the height of the ceiling and add them up:

	Length (ft.) ×	Ceiling Height (ft.) =	Area (sq. ft.)
Wall A			
Wall B			+
Wall C			+
Wall D			+

Total Wall Area = sq. ft.

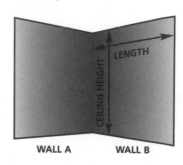

WALL A   WALL B

2 **CALCULATE THE QUANTITY OF PAINT NEEDED:**

Divide the Total Wall Area by 400 square feet per gallon to get the quantity of paint needed per coat. For rough or textured surfaces, divide by 300 square feet instead. (Note: Coverage per gallon noted above is industry standard, check the paint label for specific information.)

	Total Wall Area (sq. ft.) ÷	Coverage (sq.ft. / gallon) =	Paint Needed (gallons)
Smooth Surface		400	
Rough Surface		300	

How about windows and doors? It ususally isn't necessary deduct the square footage taken up by windows and doors in the average wall when estimating how much paint is needed to do a room. An exception would be on walls with oversized windows or with several windows or doors.

CEILINGS OR FLOORS

1 **CALCULATE THE SURFACE AREA:**

Multiply the length by the width to get the surface area.

Length (ft.) × Width (ft.) = Surface Area (sq. ft.)

2 **CALCULATE THE QUANTITY OF PAINT NEEDED:**

Divide the surface area by the coverage per gallon to get the number of gallons needed. (See Step 2 above.)

	Surface Area (sq. ft.) ÷	Coverage (sq.ft. / gallon) =	Paint Needed (gallons)
Smooth Surface		400	
Rough Surface		300	